ANCIENT CHINESE BRONZES

IN THE

AVERY BRUNDAGE COLLECTION

A selection of vessels, weapons, bells, belthooks, mirrors, and various artifacts from the Shang to the T'ang dynasty, including a group of gold and silver wares.

By René-Yvon Lefebvre d'Argencé

Published by Diablo Press for the de Young Museum Society

Preface

This book illustrates some of the most representative archaic Chinese bronzes collected over a period of more than thirty years. Their study should contribute to a better knowledge of Oriental art in one of its most esoteric developments. Hopefully, it will also foster a certain 20th-century humility from the discovery that man in a supposedly primitive society about 3000 years ago could, without modern scientific knowledge or technique, produce such masterpieces of sophisticated design and execution.

Avery Brundage

The Avery Brundage Collection is a source of great pride for the M. H. de Young Memorial Museum and for San Francisco; this book can only begin to illustrate its extent and excellence. Through perseverance and the exercise of well-informed judgment over a period of thirty years, Mr. Avery Brundage has developed a collection of unrivalled quality, a work of art in itself.

The Avery Brundage Collection adds immeasurably to San Francisco's cultural resources and makes the de Young the most comprehensive art museum in the western United States. In its position as gateway to Asia, San Francisco has long been exposed to the influence of the cultures across the Pacific. Out of this exposure grew appreciation, and it seems most appropriate that the Collection should find its home here. From it, many of our citizens will derive renewed interest in their heritage. The result of Avery Brundage's generous gift to San Francisco is certain to be a greater understanding of the arts of the Orient and, therefore, the cultural enrichment of our future generations. San Franciscans, who have supported the collection by authorizing the construction of a museum wing to house it, now have an unparalleled opportunity to share in the adventure begun by Avery Brundage.

Richard S. Rheem
President, Board of Trustees
Jack R. McGregor
Director

Ancient Chinese Bronzes is the first of several volumes designed to illustrate various departments of the Avery Brundage Collection of Oriental Art. The items shown here represent approximately one-fifth of the contents of the Department of Ancient Chinese Bronzes and related objects. Dating from 1500 B.C. to A.D. 900 they trace the technical and stylistic evolution of some of the most significant branches in Chinese art during twenty-four centuries. Our choice has been dictated by the quality of the objects and their historical interest. Although our ambition has been to include at least one or two outstanding specimens of each main category, it has seemed natural to emphasize the ancient bronze vessels for which the collection is so well-known.

I am indebted to the staff of the Oriental Department of the museum, particularly to Mr. Clarence Shangraw, Assistant Curator, Miss Huang Woan-jen and Miss Yoshiko Kakudo, Research Assistants, who have collaborated with me in all phases of preparation of this volume. Mr. William Abbenseth has spared no time or trouble in procuring outstanding photographs, and in meeting with great success the challenge of grouping several objects in the same print while maintaining unity in settings and backgrounds. Mr. Roger Broussal, Conservator of the collection, has drawn the map with his usual care and talent. Kenneth Kral designed the cover.

I am particularly grateful to Professor Alexander Soper in generously allowing me to quote from his draft of the catalogue of the mirrors in the collection. I also owe a great debt of gratitude to Mr. Avery Brundage whose suggestions have contributed in large measure to give this handbook its present form and character.

In 1963, Mr. Brundage made to the department a generous gift of more than 2,000 books and periodicals which he had collected in thirty years. His example was enthusiastically followed by the Society for Asian Art and the Marshall Steel Foundation. My thanks go to all these donors whose contributions became the nucleus of a research library of Oriental art. I would also like to express my gratitude to Dr. Elizabeth Huff and Dr. Richard Irwin of the University of California, Berkeley, for giving me free access to the East Asiatic Library.

René-Yvon Lefebvre d'Argencé
Director
Avery Brundage Foundation

CONTENTS

Preface   3

Introduction

     The History 7

     The Vessels 9

     Chronology of Early Chinese Dynasties 11

Plates

     Shang 12-65

     Western Chou 66-85

     Eastern Chou 86-111

     Han 112-121

     Warring States to T'ang Mirrors 122-125

     T'ang 126-131

Bibliography   132

Major Bronze Sites in Ancient China

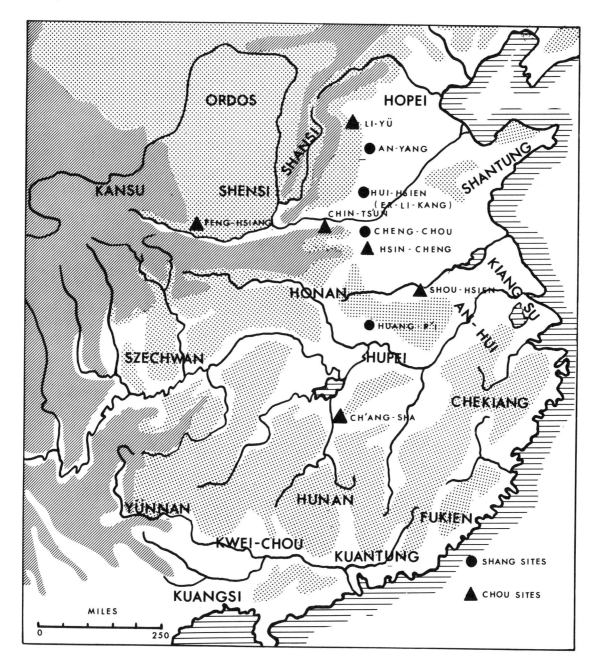

ORDOS

HOPEI

KANSU

SHANSI

SHENSI

▲ LI-YÜ

● AN-YANG

● HUI-HSIEN
(ER-LI-KANG)

CHIN-TSUN

▲ FENG-HSIANG

▲

● CHENG-CHOU

▲ HSIN-CHENG

SHANTUNG

HONAN

▲ SHOU-HSIEN

KIANG-SU

● HUANG-P'I

AN-HUI

SZECHWAN

SHUPEI

CHEKIANG

▲ CH'ANG-SHA

YÜNNAN

HUNAN

FUKIEN

KWEI-CHOU

KUANTUNG

● SHANG SITES

▲ CHOU SITES

KUANGSI

MILES

0   250

Introduction

THE HISTORY

Middle Shang period

Illustrated only by a few recent discoveries made in the districts of Cheng-chou and Hui-hsien in Honan and at Huang-p'i in Hopei or by a few chance findings (See for instance Pl. I) this period is still ill-defined. The name was not in use until a few years ago, and the scarcity of the material yielded by the mentioned sites has so far discouraged serious attempts at describing the period in more than general terms. The theory was advanced that the Cheng-chou sites with their walls of stamped earth were vestiges of the city of Ao, the second capital of the dynasty, but many specialists have objected that the remnants were too unimpressive to be associated with such a prestigious name. The question whether Middle Shang bronze vessels represent the first metallurgical experiments in China is also open. They display many technical imperfections, yet shapes and ornaments are regulated by a sense of proportion and symmetry which is hardly suggestive of an art at its beginning. The problem of dating these bronzes with some precision is very arduous. It might be mentioned that, so far, no Middle Shang, site has yielded any inscribed materials (See p.10).

The Late Shang Period

Until 1950 knowledge of the material culture of the Late Shang period was confined to the single site of Hsiao-t'un (An-yang) in Honan. Since then this knowledge has been enriched by the discovery and investigation of about eighty other sites. Today we know that the Shang culture radiated as far north as northern Hopei and as far south as Hunan. Westwards it reached the western borders of Shensi and eastwards expanded to the maritime province of Shantung.

This is the period of the culmination of Shang civilization and the rise and fall of the last dynastic capital, An-yang, whose vestiges still form our main source of information on the Shang dynasty.

Our understanding of the political and economical structures of the Shang state is very incomplete. We do not know whether it should be called a kingdom or a loose federation of fairly independent city-states. Shang society probably was split into the wealthy and powerful rulers in the walled cities, and the subjects, mostly peasants, kept in serfdom. New archaeological data seem to point to the existence of a nucleus of a class of relatively independent artist-craftsmen and merchant travelers. At this point all that can be said with some confidence is that the capital and its immediate vicinity were under the control of a monarch who exercised the highest administrative, military, and religious functions. The names of all but two of the twelve Shang rulers are mentioned in contemporary literature.

Fragments of this literature have reached us in the form of inscriptions scratched on the surface of animal bones and tortoise-shells used in divination (oracle bones) or cast on various parts of the bronze vessels. Isolated and terse as they are, these texts have shed considerable light on the cultural and religious aspects of the period. Their existence shows that Shang China was in possession of a highly developed form of script and was very history conscious. Events and occurrences were recorded for later reference.

The Western Chou

The Chou were living initially west of the Shang with whom they entertained alternately friendly and hostile relations. Shortly before the conquest, they built in the heart of Shensi the fortress cities of Feng and Hao. The latter was to remain their capital until 771 B.C. when the Chou kings exercised their power over the whole of northern China and a vast area in the south, including the provinces of Hunan and Chekiang.

Despite their military successes the Western Chou rulers did not think of themselves as emperors, but as kings. This apparent modesty reflected the actual political conditions they had created by parceling out conquered lands to their relatives and allies. This policy resulted in a feudal system, in many respects akin to that of medieval Europe.

The only texts which have survived from the early centuries of the Chou regime are inscriptions on bronze vessels. In recent years, many Chou sites have been discovered including that of the famous city of Ch'eng-chou which the new rulers built near Lo-yang in Honan, soon after their accession to power.

The Ch'un-Ch'iu period

Ch'un-ch'iu or "Spring and Autumn" is the title of a classical laconic chronicle attributed to Confucius, recording events that affected the state of Lu from 722 to 481 B.C. Lu was the birth-place of Confucius and comprised parts of present-day Shantung, Honan, Anhwei, and Kiangsu.

Toward the beginning of the 8th century B.C., a few relatively powerful feudal lords emerged from the multitude of small fiefs which had been competing with each other throughout the Western Chou period. The weakness of the central authority declined still further. The Chou lost the whole of their native Shensi and moved to Ch'eng-chou which remained the capital until the end of the dynasty.

The end of the period was marked by great cultural, particularly philosophical, activities which stimulated Confucianism and Taoism.

The Warring States

This was a period of extended battles between seven large states which shared most of the Chou territory. It also was the period of the "hundred philosophers" when "all flowers bloomed and a hundred schools of thought contended." The religious, social, and technological changes which had begun to take place during the Ch'un-ch'iu period now created patterns from which China did not depart until modern times—especially the rise of a powerful class of scholar-officials and the establishment of a culture based on a common system of writing.

THE VESSELS

The sources

The recognition of the ancient Chinese bronzes as outstanding contributions to the art of the world is fairly recent but scientific interest in bronzes is not new. Its origins can be traced to the antiquities-minded Sung dynasty (960–1279 A.D.) when several generations of scholars worked on a series of voluminous "catalogues of antiquities." At first, ancient bronzes were valued chiefly for their inscriptions, but epigraphy soon opened the way to the first typological and chronological classifications. Many class names and some special terms still in use to designate individual motifs were created or homologated by the Sung catalogers.

Several of the leading bronze specialists of the present generation are epigraphists who interpret the inscriptions which remain irreplaceable tools. Since the turn of the century, however, a series of rewarding campaigns of excavations and the adoption of scientific archaeological and art-historical methods have revived and enlarged the field. The study of the vessels themselves has become a major branch of Chinese art history. Shapes, ornamentation, and their interrelation have been the object of thorough and ever-progressing investigations. Detailed chronologies have been established. Scientists specializing in bronze casting and bronze alloys are procuring data which provide new tools for study.

The discoveries of the past fifteen years have been spectacular. They have demonstrated the existence of bronze casting in China as early as the Middle Shang period (See Pl. I), permitted the establishment of tighter chronological sequences, and shed light on the important problem of regional styles.

Metallurgy

The beginning and rapid efflorescence of a bronze industry is the most important feature of Shang China.

Bronze is an alloy of copper and tin. In the Near East, bronze was already in general use toward the second half of the 3rd millennium; the usual proportion of copper and tin was 9 to 1. West of China, the Bronze Age was frequently preceded by a period during which copper was used for tools and weapons.

In China metallurgy began directly with the casting of bronze vessels. When compared with the consistency of western alloys, Chinese bronzes are erratic. The percentage of tin varies from 5 to 20 percent, and a third ingredient, lead, also plays an important part. In finely decorated vessels (See for instance Pl. III) the introduction of lead is a technical improvement. It reduces the melting point of the alloy, facilitates the flow of the metal during casting, eliminates the formation of bubbles, and makes possible the use of minute surface embellishments. Alloys were prepared in earthenware crucibles placed over a charcoal fire. The liquid was then poured into molds also made of clay. The manufacture of vessels with many structural parts called for elaborate molds which could be made only by people with a long and advanced ceramic tradition. As for the controversy between the supporters of the direct method (multi-mold casting) and those of the cire perdue method (wax casting of the type used throughout the Bronze Age in the West) it can only be said that neither one method could have attained such a high degree of sophistication if they had not been served by the unsurpassed technical knowledge and versatile talents of the Chinese potter. In this sense, at least, Shang bronze casters are the direct heirs of the neolithic clay throwers.

Use

During the Shang and Chou dynasties bronze was regarded as a semi-precious material (See Pl. II). It was practically out of reach of the masses, and even the ruling classes restricted its use for ceremonial or military purposes. This explains why the bulk of the objects discovered so far consists of vessels, weapons, and chariot parts.

Most vessels in museums or private collections come from tombs, which accounts for their variegated patinae (See Pl. XIV-A). Some of them have been cast specifically to be interred with the dead to keep them company in their after-life. Others, among them the best Shang products, were originally made to be used in sacrifices and more particularly in the offering of foods and wine to the ancestors who, together with other deities or deified spirits, were worshiped in propitiatory and augural ceremonies. During the Chou dynasty many vessels were also cast to serve as status symbols or as tokens of the close ties between kings or feudal lords and their liege-men.

Typology

It has become customary to group vessels under three main categories according to their presumed original contents: wine, food, and water.

The following synoptic chart is based on the classification given by the K'ao Ku T'u, a late eleventh century "Illustrated Catalogue of Antiquities" in ten volumes:

Food vessels: Fu, Hsien, Kuei, Li, Ting, Tou, Tui, Yü
Wine vessels: Chia, Chih, Chüeh, Fang (Square) Yi, Ho, Hu, Ku, Kuang, Lei, P'ou, Tsun, Yu
Water vessels: Chien, P'an, Yi

During the Shang period the category of wine vessels is by far the most numerous and diversified, which seems to corroborate the Chou charge that the Shang were heavy drinkers. Chou casters produced mainly food and water vessels, a phenomenon which reflects a profound transformation in religious practices if not in social habits.

Each main category is further divided into typological classes and subclasses. Some classes, like the Ting (Pls. IV-A, V, XXVIII, XXIX, XXXIX), Kuei (Pls. XXXI, XXXIV, XXXV-B, XXXVI), Hu (XV, XVI, XXXIII-A and B, XXXIV-B, XXXV-A, XLII-B, XLIII, LXIV, XLV-A and B, LIV), Hsien (XXVII-A), and P'an (XIV-B) are represented in each phase of the evolution during the entire span of the Bronze Age. Other classes disappeared at a comparatively early stage, for instance the Chia, Chüeh, Ku, Tsun, Chih, Kuang, and Fang Yi. Others, like the Yi (XXXIV-A and XLI), Tou (LX-B), and Fu (XL-A) are late innovations. Finally, the vicissitudes of the Ho class (Pl. I-B, VI, VII, XXXVI-A and XLV-C) are typical of the revivals which affected a few types after long periods of interruption.

Inscriptions

Chou bronze bells and Han (or later) mirrors are frequently inscribed but not vessels. The high ratio of inscribed items in this selection (almost 50 percent) is unusual.

Inscriptions are seen for the first time in association with Late Shang vessels and tend to increase in size with the Chou. Early bronze casters did not allow inscriptions to interfere with surface decorations. Their preference went to the comparatively flat bottoms of some vessels or the inner side of the lids. Special devices had to be found for long-necked, coverless vessels like those of the Ku class (See Pl. X), where inscriptions are hidden inside the hollow foot. The only conspicuous exceptions to this habit are those on Ho and Chüeh tripods where two or three graphs are frequently half concealed behind the handle (See Pls. VI, VIII and also VII, which illustrates a vessel with no known counterpart). After the Early Western Chou, this rigid practice loosened gradually and inscriptions began to occur on surfaces, and, at times, in unexpected parts of the vessels (See for instance Pls. XXXV-A and XXXVI-A).

Late Shang and Early Western Chou inscriptions were frequently cast deep in the flesh of the metal with enough calligraphic dexterity to suggest models written with a brush. Later epigraphs lost much of their formal character and were cast or engraved rather casually and stiffly so that they hardly reflect the great progresses achieved by calligraphers in the course of the Ch'un-ch'iu and Warring States periods.

At first, inscriptions were laconic. They rarely exceeded two rows of three characters each. Human silhouettes which are so conspicuously absent from Shang ornaments are quite commonplace. Typical formulae mention the name of the donor—frequently called "father" or "uncle"—the name of the vessels, and the fact that it is a precious object to be preserved with utmost care. Exceptionally explicit for the period is the dedicatory formula cast on the bottom of the Rhinoceros Tsun (See cover and Pl. XIX). It consists of twenty-seven characters referring to a gift of cowries made by the king to a high official in connection with a sacrifice performed upon the king's return from a punitive expedition.

Early Western inscriptions can be even more substantial. The Square Ting illustrated in Pl. XXVIII, for instance, has thirty-three characters, and that in Pl. XXIX, thirty-two.

Old formulae are frequently kept intact until the 10th century B.C. The Yu illustrated in Pl. XXXIII has two identical 12-character inscriptions cast on the bottom and inside the cover. They can be translated freely as follows: "Uncle (also used as rank) made this perfect vessel (here called Tsun) to be cherished forever by his descendants."

CHRONOLOGY

SHANG		ca. 1523–1028 B.C.
	Middle Shang	15th-13th century B.C.
	Late Shang	13th–11th century B.C.
	(An-yang ca. 1300-1028 B.C.)	
CHOU		ca. 1027–222 B.C.
	Western Chou	ca. 1027–771 B.C.
	Early	ca. 1027–948 B.C.
	Middle	ca. 948–858 B.C.
	Late	ca. 858–771 B.C.
	Ch'un-ch'iu	770–481 B.C.
	Warring States	480–222 B.C.
CH'IN		221–207 B.C.
HAN		206 B.C.–A.D. 220
	Western Han	206 B.C.–A.D. 8
	Wang Mang Interregnum	9 B.C.–A.D. 24
	Eastern Han	25 B.C.–A.D. 220
SIX DYNASTIES		221–589
SUI		589–618
T'ANG		618–906

Note: The dates given for Shang and Western Chou are those proposed by Wang Kuo-wei, Ch'en Meng-chia and Mizuno. They are based on their reconstitution of the Bamboo Annals. All dates before 841 B.C. are subject to revision.

PLATE I

A. CHIA, Ceremonial Wine Vessel.

Middle Shang Period, Erh-li-kang Style
(15th to 13th Century B.C.)
H: 13″ D: 7⅜″   B60B45

B. LI-HO, Ceremonial Wine Vessel.

Middle Shang Period, Erh-li-kang Style
(15th to 13th Century B.C.)
H: 10″ D: 6½″   B60B1078

During the Middle Shang period, tripods predominate among wine and food vessels. All share a number of structural characteristics: a marked angularity, because each part is conceived almost as a separate entity; hollow legs; thin walls; and flat, primitive handles.

Middle Shang decor is usually confined to one or two narrow zones of animal or geometric motifs cast in thin raised lines (Chia) or in deep carving (Ho). Incisions and high relief are less common and free sculpture unknown. Here, incisions are used to delineate a "whorlcircle" on the caps surmounting the uprights of the Chia, and high relief appears on the dome of the Ho to suggest a human mask with an opened mouth.

Middle Shang iconography is best known for these bands of complex and hybrid animal forms which are well exemplified by our tripods. As a rule such designs center on a mask with protruding eyes and without lower jaw. This is the "T'ao-t'ieh" of the Sung archaeologists. The term refers to a bodiless glutton and has been retained by modern historians for lack of proper identification.

Other designs frequently seen on Middle Shang vessels are the simple, raised lines known as "bowstrings," which encircle the body, and the rows of circles which frame both zones of decoration on the Chia.

A.

B.

PLATE II

CHIA, Ceremonial Wine Vessel, Inscribed.

Late Shang Period
(13th to 11th Century B.C.)
H: 29⅝″ D: 15″   B61B11

Without departing from the basic criteria set by their predecessors, Late Shang
bronze casters established formal and decorative formulae based principally on the
integration of the various components, symmetry, anatomical distribution of the
ornamentation, and superior craftsmanship.

Probably only very few king-size vessels were ever made; each of them must have
cost a fortune. Even fewer have survived. This Chia, abnormally large, can be regarded
as an excellent example of the most ornate series of the Late Shang style in its classical
phase. It shows that after mastering all the technical difficulties inherent in the
medium, Late Shang casters gave full vent to an irresistible sculptural penchant which
led them toward more and more audacious constructions.

Here, for instance, the bird-like handle is "held" in the mouth of an animal whose
spiraling horns are treated in the round. The caps of the uprights attain monumental
dimensions, and high flanges jut out at right angles from all components of the
vessel to divide them into vertical registers while frequently serving as decorative axes.

This is an extremely voluble and versatile art: tiers upon tiers of decoration in
high relief follow one another with a minimum of interruptions and fuse into a
background of rhythmic meanders.

Note that the uprights now occupy a strictly central position, whereas in Middle
Shang times they were placed in a more frontal one. (See Pl. I-A.)

PLATE III

LI-TING, Ceremonial Food Vessel, Inscribed.

Late Shang Period
An-yang Style
(*ca.* 1300–1028 B.C.)
H: 8″ W: 8″   B60B1030

This shape stands halfway between the lobe-legged Li and the semi-spherical Ting
(See Pl. IV-A) and is of Middle Shang origin. The Late Shang iconographic
repertoire is rich in animal and geometric designs which have been isolated and
classified. These designs are rarely interchangeable. Since Shang bronze art
was essentially a religious art, each class of vessels served a particular ceremonial
function, which largely dictated its shape as well as the distribution and nature of its
ornamentation. Each vessel bears a symbolically and visually coherent decor. Zones of
decoration are all at once conceived in relation to one another and with the formal
characteristics of the surface where they appear. For instance, these large masks are so
well adapted to their support that they could be called "lobe masks" (See also Pl. VI).

Late Shang decor combines frontality and motion. Each pattern in a given zone
is individualized and rhythmically connected with all other patterns in the same
zone. (See for instance the circular motion which animates the row of "whorl circles"
and "square and crescents" on the neck zone.) In this particularly fine specimen the
meander background plays an important part in the over-all composition and rhythm.

PLATE IV

A. TING, Ceremonial Food Vessel.

Late Shang Period, An-yang Style
(1300 B.C.–1028 B.C.)
H: 7⅜" D: 6½"   B60B797

B. YÜ, Ceremonial Wine Vessel.

Late Shang Period, An-yang Style
(ca. 1300–1028 B.C.)
H: 5¾" D: 7"   B60B34

(A) The belly of this sturdy Ting is covered with a geometrical pattern made of five rows of bosses against a background of lozenges. The neck zone is divided into six panels by short flanges. In each panel a crested dragon with its head turned back rises from a setting of spirals. The decoration stops short of the mouth rim and the bottom.

(B) The Yü is probably the least complicated of all Late Shang innovations. In this case at least, Shang casters certainly looked back to ceramic prototypes to cast in metal the same stem cup that clay modelers had produced from time immemorial. Because of its silhouette and type of ornamentation, this class is sometimes regarded as a subcategory of the Kuei class (See Pl. XXXI). Dragons share with "T'ao-t'ieh" the first place in Late Shang ornamentation. They constitute ideal motifs for the central zone of certain vessels, but are also found in great number on secondary or even tertiary zones. In fact, these two leitmotifs, T'ao-t'ieh and dragons, at times are linked to the point when they cannot be clearly separated. Seen at a certain angle, this vessel will seem to bear only T'ao-t'ieh masks with curvilinear extensions. Seen at another angle, it will offer a series of dragons represented in profile. This ambiguity was certainly quite intentional and is usually due to the fact that two dragons placed antithetically are liable to form a frontal T'ao-t'ieh mask. It is quite in keeping with the hybridity mentioned above, and with it denotes religious and artistic visions far more complex and sophisticated than those generally associated with ancient societies.

Just as there is a wide variety of T'ao-T'ieh masks, dragons appear in various shapes, movements and positions. This Yü gives us a particularly enlightening, if somewhat limited, illustration of the ability of Late Shang decorators to elaborate on basic decorative themes.

A.

B.

PLATE V

TING, Ceremonial Food Vessel, Inscribed.

Late Shang Period
(13th to 11th Century B.C.)
H: 14" D: 9½"   B60B1006
Published: *Sekai Kōkogaku Taikei,* Vol. 6, Page 64, Fig. 166

This Ting vessel is one of the most striking illustrations of the sculptural vein
which prevailed during the Late Shang period. Here, the container is
overpowered by massive vertical handles and by the three monumental birds which
have taken the place of the classical cylinders (See Pl. III). Birds occupy an important
place in Shang decorative morphology along with quadrupeds, reptiles, insects, and
hybrid animal shapes. The ones shown here are fairly exceptional because they look as
if they could be found in a manual of ornithology. As a rule, the Shang menagerie
is typically hybrid, partly because of the artists' desire to reduce shapes to a common
rhythm and partly because of their intricate vision of the universe. Shang artists
frequently isolated parts of an animal shape—a head, a body, a tail, a pair of legs—only
to combine them with alien components. Examples of simple juxtaposition are not
rare. More frequently, however, the various components are distorted by a
linear cadenza that blends them together and makes proper identification difficult.

PLATE VI

HO, Ceremonial Wine Vessel, Inscribed.

Later part of Late Shang Period
(12th–11th Century B.C.)
H: 11" D: 9¾"   B60B78

In classical Late Shang art all traditional vessels undergo complex structural transformations. These reflect an expression of maturity, but also result from a blending of shapes in order to form unified sets of vessels to be used conjointly.

In this respect, the Ho class is particularly enlightening. When the general contours of Middle Shang prototypes are respected (See Pl. I-B), every single component has been reshaped or replaced for a better integration of the various parts. Now the S-shaped lobes of the body fuse into smooth, solid legs, the lid is movable and attached to a bow-shaped sturdy handle by a three-link chain, and the spout has been lowered from its original high position to the shoulder of the vessel.

On the body the main motifs are contrasted against a crisp meander background. The neck zone contains six fanged dragons in profile. The same kind of fangs can be observed in the three huge masks which decorate the lobes. The masks have elongated horns which suggest silkworms (Compare with Pl. III.)

Various dragons spiral around the lid—one of them is very large and seems to be biting its tail. The spout is incised with four rising blades and a band of barbed C-shapes. Similar shapes adorn the handle which is surmounted by a bovine head in the round.

PLATE VII

HO, Ceremonial Wine Vessel, Inscribed.

Late Shang Period
(13th to 11th Century B.C.)
H: 7¾″ D: 5½″   B60B9995
Published: B. Karlgren, *BMFEA* no. 21, Pl. 12 no. 2, and
Jung Kêng, *Shang and Chou Bronzes* Vol. 11, Pl. 644

If this unusual shape can be assigned to the Ho category, it is mainly because of its
spout. The belly is not decorated. The cover, neck, and feet are divided into four panels
with a meander background. The main motifs, gaping and turning dragons with a
double tail, are repeated in each zone of decor. As in the preceding specimen, four
rising blades and a band of barbed spirals are incised in the spout. The upper part of
the handle consists of a free-sculptured bovine head with large horizontal ears. In
addition to two small vertical lug handles, the neck zone is equipped with a loop. The
latter was probably connected by a chain to a similar loop on the lid.

Portions of the cloth in which the vessel was wrapped before burial have become
an integral part of the patina. The traces of red pigment in the lines of decoration
are remnants of an application of coloring.

PLATE VIII

A. CHÜEH, Ceremonial Wine Vessel.

Late Shang Period
(13th–11th Century B.C.)
H: 9″ D: 7¼″   B60B1026

B. CHÜEH, Ceremonial Wine Vessel, Inscribed.

Late Shang Period
(13th–11th Century B.C.)
H: 7½″ D: 5½″   B60B723

Structurally speaking, the Chüeh, another wine vessel of ancient origin, is closely related to the Chia (See Pls. I-A and II). Yet it has often baffled experts as the only decidedly asymmetrical vessel of the Shang repertoire. Its elongated channel-like spout, its "tail," and the relative position of its legs pose problems still unsolved.

(A) This vessel is a typical example of the class. The deep body has regular contours. The spout and tail are of equal bulk and fuse smoothly into each other. The pillars of the uprights are flat on one side and semicircular on the other as though they were halves of a rod. The inner sides of the triangular legs are deeply grooved. The ornament is so fine that it is more suggestive of chiselling than of casting. It consists primarily of two dissolved T'ao-t'ieh masks on the belly and of rising blades inscribed with dragons or animal shapes on the spout, tail, and neck zone.

(B) This specimen is atypical. The spout, neck, and body are covered with an unusual uni-decor done in dense thread-like technique. Its spout is crowned by a single upright rising vertically from a V-shaped support. Contrary to the rule, the handle is plain, and its lower extremity does not mark the border of the decorated area. Furthermore, there is no place for the usual inscription behind the handle.

A.

B.

PLATE IX

CHÜEH, Ceremonial Wine Vessel With Lid, Inscribed.

Later part of Late Shang Period
(12th–11th Century B.C.)
H: 9¼" D: 7¾"   B60B1049

This is an unusual vessel—covered Chüeh are very rare. The lid of this one with its bovine head in the round has no counterpart, nor have the caps of the uprights in the shape of coiling snakes. Other anomalies are an incised cicada behind the handle and a cast inscription inside the body and on the verso of the lid. As a rule, inscribed Chüeh carry their inscriptions behind the handle or on the pillars of the upright (See Pl. VIII-A).

The surface decoration, heavily corroded, is framed by curious ridges with a triangular cross section and engraved chevrons. It consists of animal shapes in low relief against a background of meanders in raised lines, dragons on the lid and belly, an unusual dragonized cicada under the spout, and blades on the neck and legs.

The small animal head on the handle is a conventionalized reduction of the bovine mask on the lid.

PLATE X

KU, Ceremonial Wine Vessel, Inscribed.

Late Shang Period, An-yang Style
(1300–1028 B.C.)
H: 11¾" D: 6¼"   B60B777

This Late Shang wine goblet has Middle Shang ancestors. Such goblets are frequently found in association with the Chüeh-tripod, and, like it, ceased to be produced shortly after the downfall of the Shang dynasty. This specimen shows iconographic and technical similarities with the Chüeh illustrated Pl. VIII-A. The vessels may have been made as parts of a set.

In its fully mature phase, this beaker is usually divided into three main zones of decoration corresponding to its three main structural components, the trumpet, the frequently bulging central part that marks the bottom of the receptacle, and the hollow foot. On the more elaborate vessels, like this one, two collar zones appear at the base of the trumpet and at the top of the foot. In the main zones the decorative associations are surprisingly consistent in the whole series; usually rising blades for the trumpet and variants of the familiar T'ao-t'ieh mask for the central and foot zones. Conversely, the collar zones often show minute reptiles or insects (here: snakes and cicadae) treated in the plane and crawling along.

Most vessels of this class exhibit cruciform perforations at the base of the central zone. Some authors see in them marks left by casting tools; others conjecture some symbolic connotation. These perforations appear not only on a number of bronze vessels but also on contemporary and earlier ceramic counterparts.

PLATE XI

TSUN, Ceremonial Wine Vessel.

Late Shang Period
(13th to 11th Century B.C.)
H: 14" D: 13¼"   B60B963
Published: Jung Keng, *Shang and Chou Bronzes*
Vol. II, Pg. 260, Plate 495

The Sung cataloguers used this class as a refuge for a variety of shapes not easily placed in their system. The current cataloguing usage is only slightly more fastidious since it groups at least four classes of vessels with little in common beyond an enormously flaring lip and a swelling body.

Our example represents the oldest and most distinctive series. This is the only kind of Tsun to be attested in discoveries from the Middle Shang period. Tall, with an average height of one foot, combining a circular cross section with an angular profile reminiscent of some Lung-shan black potteries, this type is furnished with a wide shoulder zone, decorated with three bovine masks in high relief.

From mouth rim to foot, the vessel is divided into six decorated areas, the decor standing against the usual meander background. The belly and foot zones have large, crested dragons with protruding eyes. When seen at a different angle, these dragons become parts of an elongated T'ao-t'ieh mask (See Pl. IV-B). The shoulder belt is filled with dragon figures of a different type. The lip zone is adorned with a row of rising blades inscribed with two confronted vertical dragon shapes. For contrast with this otherwise uniform ornamental scheme, the base of the trumpet shows four fairly realistic long-tailed birds, and the upper belly zone contains four elongated "eye motifs."

Scored flanges divide the shoulder, belly, and foot into six panels. They serve as frames or axes for the decoration depending upon the angle at which the vessel is observed.

PLATE XII

A. FANG I, Ceremonial Wine Vessel.

Late Shang Period
(13th to 11th Century B.C.)
H: 7½″ W: 4″   B60B997

B. CHIA, Ceremonial Wine Vessel.

Later part of Late Shang Period, An-yang Style
(*ca.* 1300–1028 B.C.)
H: 9″ D: 6½″   B60B96
Published: B. Karlgren
Some Characteristics of the Yin Art, BMFEA
No. 34, 1962, Plate 36-b.

During the last centuries of the Shang dynasty, casters created massive, square, or squarish bodies, very different from the rounded volumes of former ages. Many quasi-cubic variants appear in a number of vessels and seem to bear the mark of the carpenter's square rather than that of the potter's wheel. This phenomenon reflects a gradual disentanglement of bronze-casting techniques from their ceramic origins. It may also be the expression of a new aesthetics dictated by wood carvers who occupied undoubtedly a prominent position in Shang artistic life.

(A) Fang I means simply "square sacrificial vessels." The particular shape originated early in the An-yang period and may have inspired all later square derivations regardless of classes. The bottom on the inside box is on a level with the upper part of the foot zone, and all An-yang specimens have four semicircular openings in the middle of the base. The decor of this class is extremely conservative. Usually there are large T'ao-t'ieh masks on central zones and cover, and dragons on upper body and foot zones. Some of the earliest vessels are framed by scored and notched strips which some authors regard as possible prototypes for regular flanges.

(B) As one of the three subtypes of the Late Shang Chia series, the "Fang Chia" or "Square Chia" is a latecomer equipped with a fourth leg and a flat lid topped by innocent-looking creatures which introduce a note of freshness, if not playfulness, into an otherwise austere environment.

A.

B.

PLATE XIII

CHIA, Ceremonial Wine Vessel, Inscribed.

Later part of Late Shang Period
(12th to 11th Century B.C.)
H: 11″ W: 7½″   B60B1019

After the traditional hipped cylinders with a flaring mouth (See Pls. I-II) and the rectangular subtype illustrated on the preceding plate, here is another Late Shang version of the diversified Chia series. It is characterized by a rounded, bulging body with a profile in S-shape and very sturdy legs.

This is our last example of tripods equipped with uprights, (See Pls. I, II, VIII, and IX). In all these vessels the relative position of the legs, handle, and uprights suggests that the latter may have been used as extra handles to help tilt the vessel in a type of ceremonial requiring the participation of at least two officiants.

The body of this vessel comprises three main zones of decoration, two of which are divided into six panels by three ridges alternating with three "seams." On the neck belt each ridge forms the axis of a T'ao-t'ieh shield which is flanked by "trunked dragons." On the belly zone the ridges serve as axes for T'ao-t'ieh masks which are made of two dragons in profile. The lip zone and the outer sides of the legs carry rising and hanging blades. The flat lid is topped by a pair of almost comical birds. Placed back to back, they are done in the round but have flat sides. The periphery of the lid is decorated with a narrow belt of four eye motifs alternating with a pattern of triangles and spirals. The heavy caps of the uprights have the shape of inverted beakers and are covered all over by a variety of geometric designs.

The massive handle is surmounted by a large, bovine head.

PLATE XIV

A. P'OU, Ceremonial Wine Vessel.

Late Shang Period, An-Yang Style
(*ca.* 1300–1028 B.C.)
H: 6¼" D: 13"   B60B1001

B. P'AN, Ceremonial Water Vessel, Inscribed.

Late Shang Period An-yang Style
(ca. 1300–108 B.C.)
H: 6" D: 15"   B60B1018

(*A*) The P'ou is an early shape, perhaps of Middle Shang origin, which shows close affinities even with other classes such as the Tsun or the Lei, but can be distinguished from all others by the unusual length of its body diameter and its rather squat appearance. Bronze alloys of the type used by the ancient Chinese are highly sensitive to earth or air chemicals. No Shang-vessel has preserved its original surface. Some vessels have developed smooth jade-like patinae with attractive encrustations which have largely contributed to their popularity among Western collectors. On such unsoiled vessels one can best study the meanders, spirals, and geometric assemblages which constitute the agitated background ornamentation of so many Late Shang series. One of the most popular background patterns, the same which fills in all the available space on the neck and body bands of this P'ou, struck the Sung archaeologists as particularly violent. They likened it to the character for "thunder" in ancient Chinese.

(*B*) After the Ho, Chia, Chüeh, Ting, Li-Ting, Tsun, and Ku, the P'an is the eighth and last class of vessels of Middle Shang origin. It also happens to be the only Shang water vessel. The originality of the P'an decor lies in a vivid contrast between the vessel's outside surface, which remains rather commonplace in its hieraticism, and its inner surface, which displays on a plain background a set of animal motifs treated in a gentle, almost naive manner. This is an unexpected and refreshing corner of the otherwise rather formidable Shang decorative palette. The inner surfaces of most P'an basins are adorned with aquatic or amphibian creatures gyrating around a central turtle. Others, like this one, combine in a more global vision this aquatic fauna with quadrupeds and birds. This is one case where the usually highly sophisticated Shang bronze art seems to yield to more popular tastes.

P'an were perhaps reserved for ablutions in which not only the officiants, but also some of their assistants, took an active part.

B.

A.

PLATE XV

HU, Ceremonial Wine Vessel.

Later part of Late Shang Period
(12th to 11th Century B.C.)
H: 14″ W: 9″   B60B6+

Pear or bottle-shaped wide containers are common from the Late Shang period, but both this vessel and the following one (Pl. XVI) present features which make them unique specimens in their respective class.

Most stout-necked Hu have two to six zones of decor with T'ao-t'ieh masks as main motifs. Here also the broad sides of the vessel bear masks, but these are atypical and become legible only when the vessel is examined upside down. These masks which invade most of the available surface appear in high relief against a meander background in raised lines and are covered with a close-knit pattern of incised barbed spirals. They show bare teeth and the embryo of lower jaws. They are crowned by enormous U-shaped horns terminating in spiraling knobs and enclosing a life-size cicada with flattened, conventional legs.

On the narrow sides of this oval vessel vertical dragons confront each other on either side of a ridge.

The vertical lug handles are remarkably small and incised on each side with a single, barbed C-shape.

PLATE XVI

YU, Ceremonial Wine Vessel.

Late Shang Period
(13th to 11th Century B.C.)
H: 14¾" D: 6¾"   B60B1008
Published: B. Karlgren, *"Some Characteristics of the Yin Art,"*

BMFEA, No. 34, 1962, Plate 56-a

This type of Yu is wholly derivative—without its swing handle and cover it could not be told from the standard bottle-shaped Hu.

From neck to foot the body shows four main horizontal zones of decor. These are divided into panels by the handle and conspicuous but plain ridges. So far as the shoulder and belly zones are concerned, these ridges serve as axes for the familiar association between T'ao-t'ieh and dragons. The foot ridges form the central part of a shield-like mask.

Each animal band is framed by a narrow belt of spirals—an unusual feature. Such a belt appears also on the border of the close-fitting lid which is topped by a bird-shaped knob.

The contours of the massive key-hole-shaped handle are accentuated by a scored central flange. This handle terminates in free-sculptured bovine heads with "bottle" horns. The underside of these heads have cavities which fit over tenons attached to the body. One side of the handle is linked to the lid through an elaborate device consisting of two rings, a free-sculptured cicada, and a movable curled-up dragon whose body encircles the pillar-like support of the bird.

PLATE XVII

CHIH, Ceremonial Wine Vessel, Inscribed.

Late Shang Period, An-yang Style
(1300–1028 B.C.)
H: 6¾″ W: 5″   B60B657

This vessel shows a number of iconographic and technical analogies with the Chüeh illustrated in Pl. VIII-A and the Ku illustrated in Pl. X. Like them, it represents the products of some of the most sophisticated An-yang workshops and is characterized by unusually well-studied proportions, by a profusion of fine details, and by the crispness of the casting.

According to traditional nomenclature the Chih is—after the Chia, Chüeh, and Ku—the fourth and last class in the group of vessels for drinking wine. It is also the last one to have appeared. Contrary to the other three shapes, it has no Middle Shang ancestor, and it is not certain that the word "chih" designated this particular shape before Sung time. In fact the vessels belonging to this class are nearly all marginal and can be distinguished from some Hu and Tsun only because the diameter of their bulging bellies is longer than that of their flaring lips (See also Pl. XVIII-A).

Lid and body are divided into four panels by segmented flanges which serve as axes for the decor. There are five zones of decoration from cover to foot. As usual, the dissolved T'ao-t'ieh on the cover and the belly zone are repetitive—so are the spiral bands on the neck and foot. The central T'ao-t'ieh mask has dragon-shaped horns. Its eyes look like the heads of wingless birds. The lip zone is adorned with a row of rising blades inscribed with a pattern of spirals and triangles.

PLATE XVIII

A. CHIH, Ceremonial Wine Vessel, Inscribed.

Later part of Late Shang Period, An-yang Style
(12th to 11th Century B.C.)
H: 7½″ W: 5″   B60B3+

B. Double-OWL YU, Ceremonial Wine Vessel.

Later part of Late Shang Period
(12th to 11th Century B.C.)
H: 7½″ W: 18″   B60B336

These vessels belong to different categories but reflect at various levels the same late twelfth- and early eleventh-century B.C., tendency toward a zoomorphic development of old shapes. This can be regarded as a phase in the trend toward more plastic effects mentioned above (See Pl. V). Of all birds, the owl was particularly popular with Shang artists, perhaps because of the dimensions of its staring eyes. Owl-shaped containers form the bulk of zoomorphic vessels.

(A) The Chih seems to represent an initial stage when the original contours of the body are not modified, nor is the lid affected. The protruding mask which occupies the central part of each broad side offers the same sort of ambiguity as the one contained in the fusion of T'ao-t'ieh and dragons (See Pl. IV-B). Seen full face, it suggests the upper part of the head of a goggle-eyed owl, but seen at a different angle it splits into two parts; each half becoming the head of a bird in profile.

(B) The Double-Owl Yu—or Tsun, for here the terminology is rather hesitant—is more explicit without attaining downright zoomorphism. The vessel is transformed from top to bottom, including the legs, into two addorsed owls. The only section to resist the invasion is the roof-shaped cap of the lid. Even the open-worked ears of this lid are suggestive of beaks. Note the blending of conventional and realistic details; also the taut equilibrium which prevails in the posture of these birds. Both features are typical of Shang animal art. It would seem that in such instances, Shang artists were striving to depict latent animal energy rather than realistic exteriorizations of animal life.

B.

A.

PLATE XIX
See cover.

TSUN, Ceremonial Wine Vessel, In the Shape of a Rhinoceros, Inscribed.

Later part of Late Shang Period
(*ca.* 11th Century B.C.)
H: 9″ L: 13″   B60BI+
Published: S. Mizuno, *Bronzes and Jades of Ancient China*
1959, Plate 70–71.

Wholly zoomorphic vessels are rare during the Shang period, and the present rhinoceros has no known counterpart. Rhinoceri are rarely represented in Shang art either in graphic or plastic form and; besides, this beast has no surface motifs of the usual type. If it were not for the rotundity of its belly and muzzle and for the linear treatment of its magnified eyes, one might be tempted to think that for once a Shang caster was unable to avoid the pitfalls of naturalism. The figure is a convincing illustration of latent, ponderous animal energy. The artist has dramatically succeeded in conveying the impression of a suspended motion through a careful study of the relative positions of the body, legs, neck, and ears. The animal has no tail. The missing cover was probably dome-shaped and just as plain as the rest of the vessel. According to a well-substantiated tradition this vessel was discovered near Shou-chang in Shantung in 1843 and remained in the possession of lineal descendants of Confucius for a few generations.

The 27-character inscription cast in the bottom records events which occurred toward the end of the Shang dynasty. (See Introduction, p.11)

PLATE XX

KUANG, Ceremonial Wine Vessel.

Later part of Late Shang Period
(12 to 11th Century B.C.)
H: 9″ L: 9″   B60B1032

The stylistic development of the Kuang or Ssu-Kuang, a latecomer in Shang bronze art, is dominated by audacious combinations of quadrupeds (usually bovine or ovine creatures) and birds (frequently owls).

   This Kuang is an example of the most conservative and possibly earliest series, where the boat-shaped body seems to be derived from a combination of such classical shapes as the Yü (See, for instance, Pl. IV-B) and the Chüeh (See Pls. VIII and IX). The central theme is apparent on the lid and handle alone. The belly and foot zones show familiar ornamental schemes against a background of spiral filling. The lid, neck, and spout are adorned with a profusion of small animals or animal shapes treated in a wide variety of manners ranging from quasi-naturalism to high-flown abstraction. Note, for instance, the hare (lid) or the snake-trunked elephant (neck belt) in the midst of conventionalized dragons. The "quadruped" in front of the cover is reduced to a massive head and a flange-like mane which curls up at the end. The thick-lipped mouth shows bare teeth. The horns are bottle-shaped, and the small ears project at right angles from the temples. Its counterpart, the bird, is also reduced to a mask still reminiscent of a T'ao-t'ieh with dragon-shaped horns in the round. The intention of the artist is best revealed by the powerful free-sculptured beak which underlines the movement of the mane and probably served as a handle to lift the cover.

PLATE XXI

A. KUANG, Ceremonial Wine Vessel, Inscribed.

Late Shang or Early Western Chou Period
(11th to 10th Century B.C.)
H: 12½" L: 15"   B60B1004

B. KUANG, Ceremonial Wine Vessel, Inscribed.

Late Shang or Early Western Chou Period
(11th to 10th Century B.C.)
H: 9¾" L: 11"   B60B976

In their search for vivid illustrations of the theme discussed in the preceding example, Late Shang casters produced Kuang vessels which contained the essential of the original message to the exclusion of secondary features. One difficulty was to strike a balance between birds and quadrupeds. These vessels represent only two among a wide range of compromises.

(A) Despite minor modifications the cover resembles that of the preceding specimen, and so does the tripartite division of the body and the use of spiky flanges. This vessel is noteworthy for its squarish shape, its huge composite handle, and its long-beaked, long-crested, long-tailed bird whose spiky silhouette is repeated sixteen times on lid, body, and foot zones.

(B) The front mask on the lid and the head on the handle are distinctly ovine. The rear mask on the lid terminates in a small free-sculptured bird. The vessel has lost its tripartite division as well as its meander background so that the birds which constitute the bulk of the decoration appear in low relief on a plain surface. Most of the body and part of the foot band are occupied by a large bird in profile. It has a thin spiraling crest, a protruding eye, and a lean leg with an elongated spur. Its most surprising feature is its large, conventional tail, which is adorned with two quills. Diminutive and simplified versions of this bird appear on the lid and the foot. The region of the body next to the handle bears thin-bodied "gaping dragons."

A.

B.

PLATE XXII

A. CHARIOT OR HARNESS FITTING WITH RATTLES.

Late Shang dynasty, An-yang Style
(1300–1028 B.C.)
H: 3½" L: 12½"   B60B826

B. CH'I, Dagger.

Late Shang dynasty, An-yang Style
(1300–1028 B.C.)
L: 11¼"

C. TOU, Pipe-Shaped Wine Ladle.

Late Shang Period
(13th to 11th Century B.C.)
L: 8"   B60B624

The decorations of a number of small ceremonial or semi-utilitarian objects are similar to those of the vessels.

(A) Some of them are still awaiting proper identification, such as many chariot or harness parts which so far have always been found isolated from their original context. This object, for instance, is also known as a harness piece or a bow-shaped ornament. Its decorative motifs are embellished by insets of turquoise, a stone which was much in favor with Shang and Chou lapidaries.

(B) The row of cicadae and whorl circles on the blade of this knife is reminiscent of the neck bands of some classes of vessels, but in the best Shang spirit the decorations are perfectly adapted to the available triangular space. Such knives are the prototypes of the earliest pieces of money, and the undecorated ones may have been produced in sufficiently large numbers to have served, themselves, as currency.

(C) The liquids in the bronze vessels were decanted by ladles. One type of Kuang mixers was conceived in function of an inner ladle, the handle of which was partly projecting from the rear of the vessel as a sort of tail. It is possible that this spoon served this purpose. It consists of a truncated egg-shaped measure and of a sculpted, double-bent handle.

A.

C.

B.

PLATE XXIII

YÜEH, Axe.

Late Shang Period
(13th to 11th Century B.C.)
H: 8″ W: 5″   B60B790

Tanged axes are among the most characteristic weapons of the Early Bronze Age in China. Used initially as battle axes, Yüeh became later ceremonial weapons and may have been used in human sacrifices.

Blades are large, often asymmetrical, and tangs are frequently off-center. The tang was inserted in a slot in a wooden shaft from which the blades projected at right angles.

In this specimen the axe was secured to its shaft by thongs laced through a central hole and two slits at the base of the blade. The fourth perforation at the top of the tang may have served as a suspension device.

The upper part of the tang is decorated in intaglio with an animal shape inscribed in a square. The figure is deeply countersunk and was probably inlaid with turquoise or some other semiprecious stone.

The blade shows a large curling dragon partly in high relief and partly in openwork. The mouth is gaping and shows a pair of sturdy fangs. The body is scaled, and the spine presents T-shaped scores similar to those of the flanges of so many contemporary vessels.

PLATE XXIV

A. T'AO-T'IEH MASK.

Late Shang Period
(13th to 11th Century B.C.)
H: 6½" W: 8"   B60B64

B. FINIAL WITH MASKS.

Late Shang or Early Western Chou Period
(11th to 10th Century B.C.)
H: 6" W: 4"   B60B1025

C. FINIAL WITH MASKS.

Late Shang or Early Western Chou Period
(11th or 10th Century B.C.)
H: 6" W: 4"   B60B1024

(A) Masks were probably used in religious rites. They were fragile, and few are in existence today. Most of those that survived are such T'ao-t'ieh which seem to have escaped from some typical Late Shang bronze vessel. This one has ram's horns, C-shaped striated eyebrows with sharp edges, globular eyes with strongly accentuated pupils like those of a fish, and a fanged upper jaw. Like most fully integrated T'ao-t'ieh, it conveys an ominous or overbearing impression. The suspension holes over the horns indicate that these masks were functional objects.

(B and C) These other pieces of ceremonial paraphernalia probably served as finials for staves or poles as indicated by the presence of lateral attachment holes. They give a clue how some masks could be worn. In front, human heads are surmounted by jawless, heavily horned T'ao-t'ieh masks. On the back, large ovine masks are placed on top of smaller masks. One of the latter is suggestive of an elephant's head—perhaps a faithful rendering of some scene of shamanistic inspiration.

Man is rarely represented in early bronze art and never in a realistic way. Human faces, when shown, are distinctly ageless and sexless. The features of these particular ones are conventionalized to the point where they suggest masks rather than human faces.

A.

B.   C.

PLATE XXV

A. STAFF FINIAL, Horse's Head.

Late Shang to Early Western Chou Period
(11th to 10th Century B.C.)
H: 3¾" W: 3¾"   B60B833

B. FINIAL, Bird.

Late Shang Period
(13th to 11th Century B.C.)
H: 4" W: 2½"   B60B632

C. LINCH-PIN in Form of Buffalo Head.

Late Shang Period
(13th to 11th Century B.C.)
H: 4" W: 3"   B60B832

D. RATTLE.

Late Shang or Western Chou Period
(11th to 10th Century B.C.)
H: 6" W: 3"   B60B851

Shang and Early Western Chou casters hardly developed monumental statuary, but they produced small animal figures in the round which inspired many subsequent dynasties.

In this domain the approach of these artists varied from near-verisimilitude to abstractions, and from plain surfaces to detailed ornamental schemes. Their compositions convey a feeling of condensed, latent energy which, beyond themes, fashions, and even media, remains the outstanding characteristic of the animal art of the period.

Despite obvious differences in formats and attitudes, these four diminutive sculptures share a surprised, if not startled look. Eyes are protruding and staring, ears act as tense danger signals, and the posture of the birds is the very image of alertness.

A.

B.

C.

D.

PLATE XXVI

YU, Ceremonial Wine Vessel, Inscribed.

Late Shang or Early Western Chou Period
(11th to 10th Century B.C.)
H: 10½" W: 8¼"   B60B1021
Published: B. Karlgren, *"Marginalia on some Bronze Albums"*
BMFEA, 1959, 31, Plate 32-b.

The vessels illustrated here and in Pls. XXVIII to XXXI, show some of the main characteristics of the Early Western Chou "exuberant style." All five would belong to the Late Shang period by their structure and the distribution of their decor, but they introduce unprecedented features such as the relatively disproportionate dimensions of secondary components: bases, feet, handles, flanges, and the bird motifs.

Like most latecomers, the Yu class is essentially derivative. Eight different subcategories have been identified and practically all stem from older shapes. They all display two outstanding formal characteristics—a swing handle and a close-fitting lid of impressive size.

The subtype illustrated here is considered one of the most typical of the whole series. This Yu has an oval section. Its twisted bow-shaped handle crosses the wider axis, and its cover consists of a cupola and a slightly splaying rim which fits over an inner high concave rim. Structurally and iconographically this rim is disassociated from the cupola and is an integral part of the body as a kind of lip zone, a feature which reveals the ability of Late Shang casters to adapt drastically new features to traditional forms.

PLATE XXVII

A. HSIEN, Ceremonial Food Vessel, Inscribed.

Early Western Chou Period
(10th Century B.C.)
H: 19" D: 13"   B60B998

B. LEI, Ceremonial Wine Vessel.

Late Shang or Early Western Chou Period
(11th to 10th Century)
H: 18" W: 11"   B60B1053

(A) After the Li, Li-ting, Kuei, and Yü, the Hsien ends the series of food vessels. This is a composite steamer vessel. The lower part is an adaptation of the Li, and the higher part is a large container with a perforated base known as Tseng. Vessels belonging to this category are well attested in the neolithic pottery of the Lung-shang type, and are still today part of the equipment of any Chinese kitchen. From the Middle Shang on, as a ceremonial vessel, the Hsien is extremely conservative. The Li part is apt to be very ornate, its lobes frequently bearing enormous animal masks which assimilate the legs as nasal appendages. But the Tseng part remains staunchly reserved, with hardly more than a narrow neck band of motifs which recall the vocabulary of the Middle Shang "restrained style." This lack of homogeneity is so consistent that one can hardly speak of a stylistic evolution.

(B) This "square" Lei is another example of the "restrained style" in its transitional phase when Shang shapes and ornamentation are gradually transformed by Early Chou taste. Our vessel shows characteristics common to most Lei: the slightly "shrugging" angle formed by the shoulder handles, the conspicuous belly handle which helped to tilt the vessel, a shoulder band decorated with whorl circles and animal heads in high relief or in the round, and a contrasting neck zone which is never treated as an extension of the body.

A.

B.

PLATE XXVIII

FANG TING, Ceremonial Food Vessel, Inscribed.

From Site Near Feng-hsiang (Shensi)
Early Western Chou Period
(Dated *ca.* 1024–1005 B.C.)
H: 10″ W: 9″   B60B2
Published: Ch'en Meng-chia *"Chronology of Bronze Vessels of Western Chou," Kaogu Xuebao*
1955, 9, Plate 9, Page 168 and 1956, 1, Pl. 4.

This unique vessel was unearthed in 1924 from a royal tomb near Feng-hsiang, in Western Chou territory. Its lengthy inscription records one of the punitive expeditions marking the beginning of the Chou hegemony and specifies that the vessel had cost a hundred pair of cowries to make. Each side is divided into two panels by heavy hooked flanges. Each panel contains a bird in profile and in high relief against a background of spiral filling. These birds have large protruding eyes, S-shaped crests, and short, bending tails topped with a single quill. At each corner the beaks of two birds fuse into each other to form a shoe-shaped projection which stands out at approximately the same plane as the central flanges.

The vessel stands on four legs in the shape of birds placed diagonally. Despite minor alterations these birds appear to be free-sculptured and simplified versions of those on the body.

PLATE XXIX

FANG TING, Ceremonial Food Vessel, Inscribed.

Early Western Chou Period
(10th Century B.C.)
H: 10″ W: 8″   B60B954
Published: Ch'en Meng-chia, *Kaogu Xuebao,* 1955, 10, Pl. 11.

This vessel is an excellent illustration of the nascent Chou style in workshops where Shang traditions were still strong.

The trapezoidal body is divided into eight panels by spurred flanges. Each median flange forms the ridge of a large mask whose most characteristic feature is a pair of sinuous and flanged horns. The lines remain descriptive enough, but they have lost the firmness of earlier times, so that all four masks have an almost sagging appearance.

The columnar supports have slender legs and are topped by animal masks in high relief. These masks are placed diagonally and have short flanges with a central projection.

The handles carry a couple of confronting dragons in climbing posture.

PLATE XXX

FANG TSUN, Ceremonial Wine Vessel, Inscribed.

Early Western Chou Period
(10th Century B.C.)
H: 9⅛″ W: 7½″   B60B1022

In spite of its balance and technical perfection, this vessel reveals the stylistic hesitations which prevailed in many Early Western Chou workshops. Round at the top, it becomes square at the bottom after a succession of difficult transitions. Moreover, the flanges introduce an extra dimension—from decorative they have become structural. Instead of simply underlining the general contours as they used to do in Shang time, they now act as contour breaks with an independent life of their own.

The decor in low relief on a ground of rounded spirals nearly covers the whole vessel. The main motif is a T'ao-t'ieh mask, whose horn and cheeks are flanged. The bodies and crests of the inverted birds on the lip zone also have flange-like excrescences. The more realistic birds of the neck and foot belts are related to the ones discussed in connection with the Square Ting illustrated in Pl. XXVIII.

PLATE XXXI

KUEI, Ceremonial Food Vessel, Inscribed.

Early Western Chou Period
(*ca.* 10th Century B.C.)
H: 8¾″ W: 12″   B60B952
Published: Jung Keng, *Shang and Chou Bronzes,*
Vol. II, Pg. 157, Plate 292

The base of this Kuei is square and hollow. Cast independently, it was at one time equipped with a small oval bell hanging from the top of the cavity. This invisible musical instrument struck a note whose pitch was carefully studied for symbolic and ritual reasons. Sparse and repetitive as they are, the ornamental schemes are typical of the transitional phase. The eye motif on the foot belt is a left-over from Shang times. But the birds on the neck and the dragons on the base are distinctively Chou. Faces and bodies are only suggested whereas beaks, crests, tails, and nondescript outgrowths occupy more of the available space.

Two small ovine masks in very high relief are set on the neck belt in axial position. Throughout the Shang period this had been one of the most significant hallmarks of the class, and it was respected even by the most erratic Early Western Chou casters.

The horns of the ovine heads on the massive handles are slightly higher than the mouth rim and this again can be regarded as symptomatic of the Early Western Chou tendency to give a structural value to decorative elements (See preceding plates for flanges).

PLATE XXXII

LEI, Ceremonial Vessel.

Early Western Chou Period
(*ca*. 10th Century B.C.)
H: 18½″ D: 18″   B60B450

This monumental vessel represents an uneasy phase in the Early Western Chou period when, in Shensi, Kiangsu, or other peripheral areas, casters were trying to adapt their inherited visions to Shang norms, or vice versa. This is essentially a time of hesitations, of growing pains. To the eye accustomed to Shang classicism the vessels made in such syncretic workshops look incongruous. The shape of this vessel and the distribution of its zones of decoration are still largely dictated by Shang traditions (See Pl. XXVII-B), so are the "shrugging" handles, the whorl circles on the shoulder and the bowstrings on the neck. Conversely it bears in prominent position a design regarded as typical of the Early Western Chou, namely a row of triangular blades containing two confronting dragons placed vertically. Furthermore the "square and crescents" which used to alternate with the whorl circles on the shoulder have been replaced by dragon shapes.

PLATE XXXIII

A. HU, Ceremonial Wine Vessel, Inscribed.

Mid Western Chou Period
(10th to 9th Century B.C.)
H: 14½″ W: 7″   B60B1054
Published: *Sekai Kōkogaku Taikei*, Vol. 6, Plate 135.

B. HU, Ceremonial Wine Vessel.

Late Western Chou Period
(9th to 8th Century B.C.)
H: 10″ W: 14″   B60B1005

C. YU, Ceremonial Wine Vessel, Inscribed.

Mid Western Chou Period
(10th to 9th Century B.C.)
H: 8¾″ W: 10″   B62B146

These vessels introduce shapes and decorative motifs which seem to be completely liberated from Shang influence.

(A) The squarish Hu bears three main zones of decoration. Two tiers of scale motifs encircle the dome of the lid, and four more form a large neckband. The scales increase in size from tier to tier, and the last row is underlined by a wavy ribbon. The body is divided into eight large zones framed by wide plain bands suggesting leather trappings. Each zone contains a large flamboyant bird in profile with a protruding eye, a long tail, a bifurcated crest, and a four-clawed leg reinforced by a conspicuous spur.

(B) The decor of this slender-necked Hu is subdued for the period. It is confined to a single neck zone and to the dome of the lid. It consists of broken wavy lines with dissolved animal shapes. Two vertical lugs with central ridges project out from the neck band. There are two suspension holes at the base of the large circular lid knob, and the base shows a network of lozenges in raised lines. The life span of this elegant vessel was comparatively short, hardly more than 150 years.

(C) This squat, almost sagging Yu (See Pl. XXVI for an earlier specimen of the class) combines decorative schemes which were applied separately to the Hu vessels on the left. On the surface of the cover and body the animalistic allusions are geometricized beyond recognition, and truly zoomorphic elements are relegated to secondary positions, such as the handle and neck band.

A.

B.

C.

PLATE XXXIV

A. YI, Ceremonial Water Vessel.

Mid Western Chou Period
(10th to 9th Century B.C.)
H: 6″ W: 11″   B60B1027

B. HU, Ceremonial Wine Vessel, Inscribed.

Mid to Late Western Chou Period
(871 B.C.)
H: 24½″ W: 12″   B60B972
Published: Jung Keng, *Shang and Chou Bronzes*
Vol. II, Page 381, Plate 720.

C. LEI, Ceremonial Wine Vessel.

Late Western Chou or Early Ch'un-ch'iu Period
(9th to 8th Century B.C.)
H: 12″ D: 12″   B60B54

D. KUEI, Ceremonial Food Vessel, Inscribed.

Late Western Chou Period
(9th to 8th Century B.C.)
H: 10¼″ W: 14″   B62 B142

(A) This water vessel is the last classical shape to appear in China. It reflects the increasing importance of ablutions in Chou ceremonials starting from the later part of the tenth century B.C. The Yi is a semi-zoomorphic "sauce boat" standing on four-clawed or hooked, knotty legs and ending in an elongated channel-like spout which is reminiscent of that of the Chüeh (See Pl. IX) or Kuang (Pl. XX). It is equipped with a large bow-shaped handle terminating in an animal head which is frequently depicted biting the rim of the vessel. A large band of dragon heads with protruding eyes and intertwining necks and crests form the main design. The background is filled with raised spirals and striations which have lost the crispness and clarity of former ages.

(B, C, D) These now familiar forms (See for instance Plates XV, XVI, XXXI, and XXXII) exhibit some of the main characteristics of the nascent Late Western Chou style. Background motifs tend to disappear altogether. Anatomical divisions are maintained, but the various zones of decor become repetitious—ornamental schemes are limited and flattened out. They frequently take the form of wide bands with wave (Hu), dragon (Lei), or scale patterns (Kuei) and tend to be exclusive. In keeping with the heavy casting of these vessels, handles are very sturdy. They have a tense semicircular profile and are often equipped with free-sculptured animal heads. Noses are generally coiling upward; horns can be almost flat or take the form of twisted cones.

C.

A.

B.

D.

PLATE XXXV

A. HU, Ceremonial Wine Vessel, Inscribed.

Late Western Chou Period, Shensi Style
(9th–8th Century B.C.)
H: 13½" W: 10"   B60B1012
Published: *Sekai Kōkogaku Taikei*, Vol. 6, Fig. 136.

B. KUEI, Ceremonial Food Vessel, Inscribed.

Late Western Chou Period
(9th–8th Century B.C.)
H: 14"   B60B1056

A comparison with Hu in Pls. XV, XXXIII, and XXXIV, and Kuei in Pl. XXXI, illustrates the stylistic evolution of these two vessels from the Shang period. Bodies are sagging and appendices (such as cover knobs and handles) are fully zoomorphic and attain hypertrophic dimensions. The surface decoration is impoverished but animated by a new ponderous rhythm.

(A) The section of the Hu is that of a rectangle with rounded curves. The vessel is divided into five zones of decoration, two for the lid and three for the body. The belly is enclosed in a network of bands in flat relief pinned down at the points of intersection by triangular or conical projections. This arrangement is suggestive of leather trappings held in place by rivets. The open areas of this network are filled with dissolved animal shapes gyrating in antithetical motions around a central eye motif. Variations of this design adorn the shoulder band and the upper neck zone.

(B) This Kuei is a further and more figurative examples of the same ornamental scheme. Here, instead of being abstracted, the axial eyes form the focal points of coiling dragons. (For other illustrations of this frequent motif, see Pl. XXXIV) Emphasized by the dimensions and positions of the dragon handles, the antithetical motion is particularly explicit. It gives the impression that the whole vessel is subjected to lateral pressure.

A.

B.

PLATE XXXVI

A. HO, Ceremonial Wine Vessel.

Late Western Chou Period
(*ca*. 8th Century B.C.)
H: 6″ W: 11½″   B60B938

B. LID.

Late Western Chou Period
(9th to 8th Century B.C.)
H: 5″ W: 11½″   B60B1029

C. KUEI, Ceremonial Food Vessel.

Late Ch'un-ch'iu Period
(6th Century B.C.)
H: 13″ W: 18″   B60B13+

In a number of cases the passage from late Western Chou to Ch'un-ch'iu appears primarily as an amplification of the currents which we have noted in connection with the objects illustrated on the two preceding plates.

(A) This Ho is the last link in a chain which goes back to Middle Shang (See Pl. I). It retains some features of its ancestors including legs of the Li category, and also shows pronounced zoomorphic tendencies. The missing lid was probably in the shape of a bird in the round.

(B) The body of this Fu was practically identical with the lid shown here. By its angularity and reversability, the vessel could be regarded as the forerunner of movements which will reach maturity during the Warring States period (See Pl. XL).

(C) The "crown and handles" of this Kuei contrast with the rest of the vessel. The former looks as though it would have burst open as a result of overgrowth. The latter have an almost anecdotic significance which is well in keeping with their baroque character. The traditional spurs take the shape of small dragon-like creatures which bite the throat of the main monsters like two diminutive vampires. The broken wavy bands which run around the lid, the belly, and the pedestal are combined with C-shaped and delta-shaped elements which may have evolved from ancient animal shapes. Such motifs together with the scale bands around the neck and foot are typical of an age when hybridity and geometrization concur to create unidentifiable patterns.

C.

A.

B.

PLATE XXXVII

CHUNG, Bell, Inscribed.

Late Western Chou Period
(9th–8th Century B.C.)
H: 24½" W: 13"   B60B180

Such bells are known as Chung. Oval in section, they were suspended mouth downward and, being clapperless, were struck on the outside with a mallet or a log— a practice which has survived until the present day. Complete sets of thirteen Chung bells have been excavated. They are graded in size, and each one strikes a different note. Music played an important part in religious and court ceremonies, and bells of this type were widely in use throughout the Chou period (See also Pl. XLVI).

With the exception of the upper part of the handle this piece is simply but fully decorated. The dragons on the top and the rows of scales on the handle ring and on the narrow belts between the nipples are done in flat relief. The lower area below the nipples is nearly filled by two addorsed coiling dragons in incised lines. The central cartouche carries a dedicatory inscription.

PLATE XXXVIII

HU, Ceremonial Wine Vessel.

Late Ch'un-ch'iu or Early Warring States Period
(7th to 5th Century B.C.)
H: 13" D: 11"   B60B1009

This very unusual vessel reflects many of the changes which marked the advent of the Warring States styles. Shapes which had survived for nearly a millennium are replaced by a small set of comparatively simple ones. Casters resort more and more to stamping techniques. Decorators keep only a few of the traditional motifs, but introduce a number of zoomorphic and geometric arrangements in which the snake occupies an important place. Ornamental schemes are frequently based on the repetition of a single unit but are animated by an ebullient rhythm which relies heavily on interlacery. Late Western Chou artists had already abandoned flanges which were incompatible with the circular movements they wanted to create. Their Warring States successors will go one step further by suppressing practically all suggestions of frontality or verticality. Their usual decorative settings are narrow belts which encircle the vessels without interruption.

The upper part of this Lei which may have served in ceremonies performed for a snake deity has three such belts. The main one around the belly shows a maze of intertwined "dragon snakes." Each reptile is linked to three others. Each one has a ring foot and a tail terminating in a kind of whorl circle in high relief. The neck and shoulder belts comprise three rows of smaller serpentiform spirals. The monster masks on the shoulder are those of fantastic snakes, as clearly indicated by the scaled forehead and the presence of realistic reptiles forming horns and eyebrows.

The incised whorl circles which adorn the otherwise plain lower part of the vessel are perhaps fossils of the foot handle, which in earlier periods had been one of the hallmarks of the Lei class (See Pl. XXVII-B).

PLATE XXXIX

TING, Ceremonial Food Vessel.

Early Warring States Period, Li-yü Style
(5th Century B.C.)
H: 19" D. 26 3/16"   B61 B8+

The Li-yü style prevailed in northern Shansi for hardly more than half a century.
This covered Ting is one of the largest vessels in this series. Li-yü contours are
remarkably pure when compared with those of other contemporary styles.

    The vessel is divided into five concentric zones of unequal widths, repetitious in their
design. This design consists of spiraling and interlacing bands centering on ram
masks, seen in front view. A concern for symmetry organizes the ebullient motion. Ram
heads in high relief appear on top of the cabriole legs, but no sculptural effect has
been attempted in connection with the L-shaped handles or the suspension rings on top
of the lid.

    One characteristic of the vessels in this series is that they are never inscribed.
Another is the extensive use of granulated details.

PLATE XL

A. FU, Ceremonial Food Vessel.

Late Ch'un-ch'iu or Early Warring States Period
(6th to 5th Century B.C.)
H: 8½″ W: 14½″   B60B916
Possibly from Hsin-cheng, Honan
Published: *Sekai Kōkogaku Taikei*, Vol. 6, Plate 241.

B. TOU, Ceremonial Food Vessel.

Late Ch'un-ch'iu or Early Warring States Period
(6th to 5th Century B.C.)
H: 8″ W: 8¼″   B60B120

C. TUI, Ceremonial Food Vessel.

Early Warring States Period
(5th to 4th Century B.C.)
H: 7″ W: 9½″   B60B97

Warring States bronze casters introduced or developed a number of reversible food vessels. Spherical or rectangular in shape, they consist of two identical or quasi-identical parts, so that covers can serve as vessels. All three vessels combine loud plastic or open-work features with serpentine or vermiculous shapes which appear in flat relief and in continuous intertwining schemes.

(A) This Fu is typical of the Hsin-cheng (Honan) style which originated during the beginning of the eighth century B.C. and set the pattern for many other regional styles of the Ch'un-Ch'iu and Warring States period.

(B) This shape has a long history, for it is well attested in Lung-shang finds. As a bronze vessel, however, it was not popular before the later part of the sixth century B.C. The body shows some rather mediocre stamped decoration, but the crown and foot with their open work of interlacing snakes are superior technical achievements.

(C) This vessel stands halfway between the Tou stem cup and the spherical Tui. The twisted bands around the cover and bowl are well attested in Warring States finds, but the naive naturalism of its bird handles prefigures a typical Han attitude.

A.

B.

C.

PLATE XLI

YI, Ceremonial Water Vessel.

Early Warring States Period Li-yü Style
(*ca.* 5th Century B.C.)
H: 5⅜″ W: 8⅜″ L: 9¾″   B65B65
Published: W. Watson, *Ancient Chinese Bronzes,*
London 1962, Pl. 63a

Since Late Western Chou times (See Pl. XXXIV-A) the Yi class has traversed a wholly
zoomorphic phase, only to lose again much of its animalistic features including legs
and the head on the handle. Here, however, the contours of the vessel in the region of
the handle do suggest the rear of an animal.

This vessel has remained so far unparalleled. Its design, and more particularly the
interlacing of snakes in openwork over the spout and the rope patterns encircling
the upper part of the body and the foot, point to a northern origin, possibly Shansi or
Honan.

—92—

PLATE XLII

A. TUI, Ceremonial Food Vessel.

Late Ch'un-ch'iu or Early Warring States Period
(6th to 5th Century B.C.)
H: 8" D: 6¾"   B60B1080

B. HU, Ceremonial Wine Vessel.

Mid Warring States Period
(5th to 4th Century B.C.)
H: 18¼" D: 9⅛"   B60B974

In some northern workshops, which were probably exposed to foreign influences, the transition from the Ch'un-ch'iu period to that of the Warring States is marked by the emergence of a new technique frequently combined with figurative ornamental schemes. Gradual and peripheral as these changes are, they reflect an entirely new attitude—bronze art becomes largely pictorial if not anecdotic.

(A) This is at the same time one of the earliest specimens of the Tui class and one of the earliest illustrations of the technique in question. Vessels of this type—near-spherical, with lids and bodies almost interchangeable—were made for barely 250 years, from the late sixth to mid-fourth century B.C. Lid and body show a pattern of composite animals with dragon heads, scaled bodies, and wrench-shaped feet. This decor is done in incised lines filled with copper thread in a manner which resembles niello work and foreshadows the brilliant inlay effects of later times. (See Pl. XLIX.)

(B) Here, the metallic filling was probably replaced by an organic substance which has disintegrated after a prolonged burial so that the design appears in intaglio. From neck to foot the body is divided into four horizontal registers by narrow raised bands decorated with geometric motifs. The four main scenes are repeated within the same register but vary from one register to another. They depict fantastic carousels where hybrid creatures, including humans or semihumans, rotate in no apparent order. Some of the animals have the same peculiar wrench-shaped feet mentioned above. (See also Pl. XLIII for variations of this feature.)

B.

A.

PLATE XLIII

HU, Ceremonial Wine Vessel.

Mid Warring States Period
(5th to 4th Century B.C.)
H: 15½″ D: 10½″   B60B1075
Published: *Sekai Kōkogaku Taikei,* Vol. 6, Plate 477, Page 166.

This Hu and the following ones exemplify more elaborate and contrasting aspects of the technique shown in Pl. XLII.

The body of the "Hunting Hu" bears eight ornamental schemes which appear in flat relief and are repeated several times within the same zone. With the exception of those belonging to the lower layer, each unit is generally framed by anvil-shaped elements. Two of these units consist of conventionalized animal shapes which may have been inspired by typical Li-yü ornamental schemes (Pl. XXXIX). The top unit represents a ring-footed, crested bird which holds a wriggling bird in its beak—all other units depict mythical hunting scenes involving nearly realistic hunters and wild beasts together with dragon-like creatures and hare-headed, bird-bodied bipeds. The purely angular and geometrical scheme of the foot band strongly contrasts with the rest of the decoration. Initially all intervals and probably also the incised details were filled with a perishable and colored substance.

PLATE XLIV

A. HU, Ceremonial Wine Vessel With Cover.

Warring States Period
(5th to 4th Century B.C.)
H: 22″ D: 14″ 	 B60B30+
Published: S. Umehara *Etudes des Royaumes Combattants*,
Kyoto 1936 Pls. LXXXIII ff.

B. HU, Ceremonial Wine Vessel With Lid and Handle.

Warring States Period
(*ca.* 5th Century B.C.)
H: 12″ D: 5⅜″ 	 B60B1079

These vessels are among the earliest examples of fully mature niello work making use
of copper alloy. Although less agitated, less diversified, and done in intaglio, the
ornamental schemes of these vessels are related to those of the preceding item.

(*A*) The decor is distributed over ten horizontal bands covering the entire surface
with the exception of the foot. Each band is divided into panels by anvil-shaped frames
and shows variants of three main decorative units: turning dragons with crests,
gaping mouths, claw-shaped feet, and three-pronged vertical tails, full-bodied felines
with spiraling crests and tails, and long-tailed birds hovering over minute deer-like
creatures.

The handles are T'ao-t'ieh masks cast separately and holding large rings incised on
one side with T-shaped spirals. The lid is surmounted by four spurred rings which
can serve as supports.

(*B*) This particular shape originated toward the latter part of the sixth century and
became extinct before 400 B.C. One of its most interesting features is the sturdiness
of its articulated handle. It seems to indicate that the vessel was subjected to
considerable hardships. The surface decorations are variants of the themes discussed
in connection with the preceding vessels.

A.

B.

PLATE XLV

A. FANG HU, Ceremonial Wine Vessel.

Mid Warring States Period
(5th to 4th Century B.C.)
H: 19½″ W: 9″   B60B966

B. PIEN HU, Ceremonial Wine Vessel.

Mid Warring States Period
(*ca.* 4th Century B.C.)
H: 13¾″ W: 12½″   B60B40

C. HO, Ceremonial Wine Vessel, Inscribed.

Late Warring States Period
(*ca.* 4th to 3rd Century B.C.)
H: 8½″ W: 9½″   B60B103

D. BIRD CAGE.

Warring States Period
(5th to 3rd Century B.C.)
H: 5⅞″ W: 5⅞″   B65B62
Published: S. Umehara, *Yamato Bunka, 1959,* n° 29, Pl. XI.
Lent by Avery Brundage

These shapes and decorative arrangements are characteristic of the main trend in the evolution of Mid to Late Warring States bronzes. Some common features are the reduction of shapes to geometric formulae, the division of bodies into small units framed by plain flat bands, the use of stamped decor combined with inlay work, and a taste for gentle free-sculptured animal shapes.

(*A*) The surface of this Hu comprises twenty-nine sunken registers. Each of them is filled with a repetitious, stamped pattern representing a couple of intertwined birds inscribed in a rectangle. The birds, which are not identical, have raised contours on a background of spirals and triangles.

(*B*) The unit of decoration is repeated in full or in part forty-five times. It consists of "dragonized" S-shapes in double line.

(*C*) After an interruption of several centuries (See Pl. XXXVI-A) the Ho makes a new and lengthy appearance. This time it has definitely renounced its Li lineage to become a near spherical tripod equipped with a wholly zoomorphic spout and a swinging bow handle which may be an archaistic feature borrowed from the long disappeared Yu class (See Plates XXVI and XXXIII).

(*D*) The lid can also serve as the bottom of the cage when the latter is reversed, in which case the birds are encaged. The walls were cut from thin plaques of metal and soldered together with the bottom forming a solid box.

B.

A.

C.

D.

PLATE XLVI

A. CHUNG, Bell.

Warring States Period
(5th–4th Century B.C.)
H: 26″ W: 12″   B60S551

B. CHUNG, Bell.

Warring States Period
(5th–4th Century B.C.)
H: 14″ W: 10½″   B60B709

C. CHUNG, Bell.

Warring States Period
(4th Century B.C.)
H: 8″ W: 5″   B60B928

Structurally Warring States Chung bells remain conservative. At the most, changes affect only the handles, base lines, and nipples, thus leaving the body and its traditional divisions intact. Yet, even the most conservative examples are invaded by designs which betray the hand of Warring States casters.

(A) This bell constitutes a transition: its contours and the proportions of its components rely almost entirely on prototypes that can be traced back to the Late Western Chou period (See Pl. XXXVII), but its decor is similar to that of a typical Early Warring States bell.

(B) The decor consists of hooks and volutes for the elongated bands between the nipples, of a monster mask flanked by entwining dragons or snakes for the bottom field, and of geometrical arrangements for the top. The traditional cylindrical handle has been replaced by confronted tigers in the round. The necks of these beasts are tied together by the two halves of a double-bodied dragon-snake to form a suspension device.

(C) In the course of the following century, animal shapes have given way to geometrical designs, and handles have become trivially semicircular or oval.

Regardless of type or age the plain rectangular fields which interrupt the ornamental schemes on the upper section are sometimes used for inscriptions or independent designs.

A.

C.

B.

PLATE XLVII

CH'UN, Bell.

Warring States Period
(4th Century B.C.)
H: 34″ W: 17½″   B60B449

Popularly known as a "Tiger's Bell," this type of musical instrument is strikingly
different from those illustrated in Pl. XLVI. Some specimens belonging to this group
are not surmounted by a tiger, but by some fantastic animal or simply by a semicircular
handle. All, however, present the same basic structural features—a tall hollow
cylinder with a bulging upper part and a circular tray-like top with a vertical side and
an everted lip. The nature of the alloy, the proportions, the posture of the tiger,
the effervescence which animates its surface treatment and contrasts with the plainness
of the bell itself, all point to a southern origin.

   We know that Ch'un bells were used in the army in connection with drums. They
seem to have been in vogue at least until the beginning of the Han dynasty.

PLATE XLVIII

A. TAPIR.

Late Ch'un-ch'iu or Early Warring States Period, Li-Yü Style
H: 4" W: 7"   B60B1000

B. Water Container in Shape of Animal.

Western Han dynasty
(2nd to 1st Century B.C.)
H: 2½" L: 6"   B60B752

C. HORSE.

Late Warring States Period, Chin-ts'un Style
(*ca.* 3rd Century B.C.)
H: 2½" W: 3⅞"   B60B664

Warring States and Early Han small animal figures in the round gain in verve and diversity what they may lose in solemnity. As well exemplified here, the arrested postures of former ages and the underlying spirit that went with them (See Pl. XXV) are still appreciated but they are no longer exclusive.

(*A*) This spell-bound tapir is a particularly well preserved specimen of Li-yü animal art at its best. Its head, body and legs are covered with a maze of designs formed mainly of flat barbed scrolls on a background of spirals and triangles. Articulations are clearly marked, and each ornamental scheme is treated structurally. The lines of the waist and neck are emphasized by ribbon bands so that the animal seems to be wearing a belt and necktie.

(*B*) After the close of the Bronze Age, bronze continued to be used for the making of half utilitarian, half decorative objects, many of which were in the form of zoomorphic or semi-zoomorphic vessels. This grotesque, forceful specimen is typical of the taste which prevailed in scholarly circles during the earlier part of the Han dynasty.

(*C*) This stocky horse stands aloof from all this agitation and fantasy. After a millennium of sporadic attempts, the naturalistic trend is now on the verge of being fully accepted.

B.

A.   C.

PLATE XLIX

A. SPEAR BUTT, Bronze with Gold Inlay.

Late Warring States Period
(*ca*. 3rd Century B.C.)
H: 3¾" W: 1¼"   B60B628

B. CHARIOT FITTING, Bronze With Silver Inlay.

Late Warring States, Chin-ts'un Style
(*ca*. 3rd Century B.C.)
H: 8½" W: 4¼"   B60B702

C. SHAFT FITTING, Bronze With Silver Inlay.

Late Warring States, Chin-ts'un Style
(*ca*. 3rd Century B.C.)
H: 7¼" W: 2⅜"   B60B685

The difficult technique of decorating bronze artifacts with ribbons and thread of gold and silver was mastered as early as the later part of the Ch'un-ch'iu period. So was the art of copper and gold repoussé. Both techniques were fully developed during the 4th and 3rd centuries, B.C. Tombs of that period have yielded inlaid weapons, weapon parts, chariot fittings and even vessels. Ornamental schemes follow the taste of a period which favors geometrical patterns combining gyration and interlacery with angularity and symmetry. Rather thin at first, the inlaid areas tend to expand to the point where they take the form of wide bands covering much of the available surface. One feels that under the pressure of more precious and more ostentatious materials, bronze is gradually losing its appeal. The time is not far when it will be relegated to a mere base for gilded or painted surfaces. The Bronze Age is drawing to an end.

C.   B.   A.

PLATE L

GOLD SHEETS IN SHAPE OF MASKS AND BIRDS.

Warring States Period
(6th to 3rd Century B.C.)
A. H: 3½″ W: 5″   B60M390
B. H: 3″ W: 3 9/16″   B60M388

These ornaments were cut from thin gold foils and probably fixed in pairs over a hard core to suggest solid gold. The decor was obtained by chasing and hatching.

(A) With its two heads fusing into a legless single body, this composite creature may be an abbreviated adaptation of some Steppe Art combat scene where a tiger would be attacking a bird.

The contours are underlined by a narrow band imitating a rope pattern. The facial features of each animal are simply, but clearly indicated. The body is covered with an interlacery of animals, probably tigers and snakes.

(B) The T'ao-t'ieh mask shows one of the rare traditional motifs which were preserved almost intact by craftsmen of the Warring States period. Thus, the horns of the monster are also the tails of two vertical confronting dragons.

Here also, the contours of the mask are strongly underlined by a sinuous rope pattern.

A.

B.

A. BELT HOOK, Gilt Bronze.

Late Warring States Period
(*ca.* 3rd Century B.C.)
L: 2″ W: 1⅜″   B65B22

B. BELT HOOK, Bronze with Gold and Silver Inlay.

Warring States Period
(*ca.* 4th or 3rd Century B.C.)
L: 1¾″ W: ¾″   B65B23

C. BELT HOOK, Bronze With Silver Inlay.

Late Warring States Period
(*ca.* 3rd Century B.C.)
L: 3¾″ W: 2″   B65B18

D. BELT HOOK, Gilt Bronze With Turquoise Inlay.

Han dynasty
(206 B.C.–221 A.D.)
L: 3⅝″ W: ⅞″   B65B19

A. BELT HOOK, Gilt Bronze With Turquoise Inlay.

Western Han Period
(2nd to 1st Century B.C.)
L: 5¾″ W: 1⅞″   B66B2

B. BELT HOOK, Cast Iron With Gold Inlay.

Warring States Period
(4th or 3rd Century B.C.)
L: 9″ W: 2″   B66B3

C. BELT HOOK, Gilt Bronze.

Sarmatic Style, Han Period
(206 B.C. to 221 A.D.)
L: 9″ W: 1¼″   B66B4

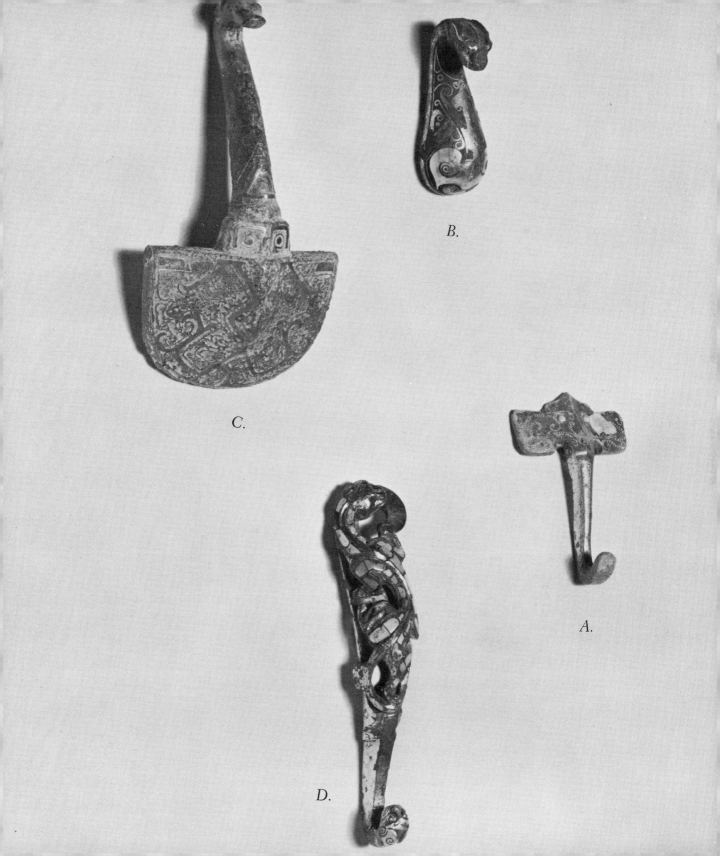

C.

B.

A.

D.

The various terms used by the Chinese to designate ancient belt hooks or buckles are transliterations from an original Hsiung-nu (Hun) word, and the introduction of these objects seems to be connected with the use of garments of nomadic origin.

Chinese texts of the early seventh century B.C. mentioned belt hooks of this type. By the fourth century B.C. they had become indispensable articles of military and more particularly cavalry equipment. Henceforth, and for half a millennium, they were produced in vast quantities. Most consist of a body terminating in a hook on one end, and, on the back of the other extremity equipped with a short-shanked button. The hook was connected to a loop, generally of perishable material, although metallic and jade loops have been found. The button could be inserted into a button hole or into a slit in a strap or belt. The object could be used as a belt hook, or as a clasp fastening different parts of a garment, or again as a suspension device for weapons or other articles of equipment.

Belt hooks were made in a wide variety of shapes and motifs. Some are cast in plain bronze or iron, or in bronze or iron inlaid with gold, silver, and turquoise. Others are gilded; solid gold or silver specimens are rare but not exceptional. At first, Chinese craftsmen borrowed themes and style directly from Steppe-Art prototypes where naturalism and narrative characterization reigned supreme, but by the beginning of the Han dynasty northern influences were eliminated gradually by the overpowering Huai style, and the sinization was complete. Hooks frequently take the shape of the head of a dragon, snake, or bird.

The motif in Plate LI-A has been interpreted as a "dolphin-like animal" or as a "long-necked bird with outstretched wing." It might also be a Chinese adaptation of an elephant's head of Ordos origin.

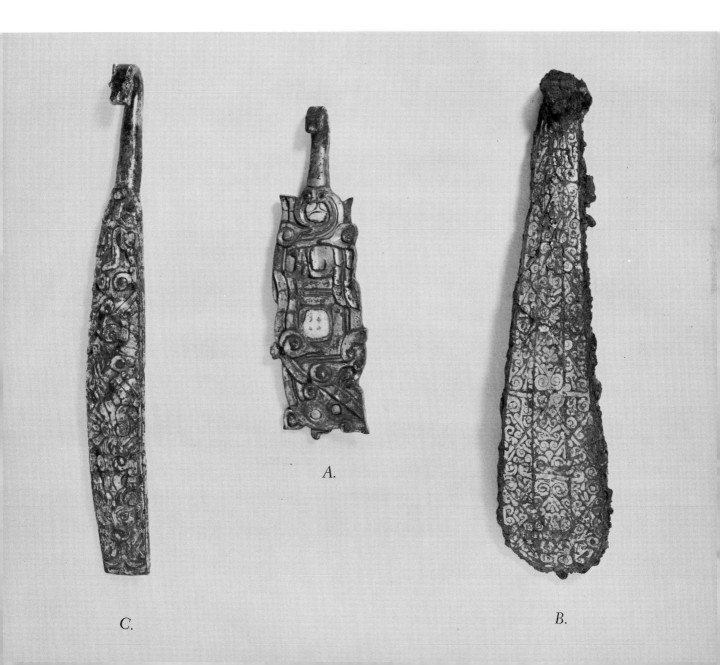

C.   A.   B.

PLATE LIII

A. LIEN, Toilet Box, Gilt Bronze.

Warring States to Western Han dynasty
(*ca.* 3rd to 1st Century B.C.)
H. 11" D: 7¾"   B60B953

B. LIEN, Vessel, Gilt Bronze.

Han dynasty
(206 B.C. to 221 A.D.)
H: 5" D: 6½"   B60B951

These cylindrical boxes mounted on three short animal legs toll the knell of Great Sacred Bronze Art such as it was practiced since the Shang dynasty. Simultaneously, they herald a new age and spirit, where the now almost profane material is being used freely for household utensils of quality. The surface of many of the vessels is left quite plain. Here *(B)* however, the artist has wrung from a metal base all he could to satisfy his irresistible pictorial urge and there *(A)* one can almost feel the cursive touch of a painting brush.

The landscape which runs almost continuously around the shorter Lien is of particular interest. It can be regarded as one of the earliest and finest sources for the study of landscape painting in China. Hunters, wild beasts, genii and mythological animals are chasing each other, against a background of wavy mountains. The scene is still imbued with the kind of mythological connotations which were so apparent on "Hunting Hu" (See Pls. XLII and XLIII) but it is also almost completely liberated from the staunch hieraticism of former ages.

Conversely other features such as the frozen T'ao-t'ieh on the body and lid of the Lien are discreet reminders of the fact that in China a deep-rooted tradition can linger on in withered conditions for many centuries.

A.

B.

PLATE LIV

HU, Ceremonial Vessel, Bronze With Gold Inlay.

Late Han dynasty
(*ca.* 2nd Century A.D.)
H: 13½″ D: 9″   B65B66
Probably From Lo-lang Area
Lent by Avery Brundage

The Hu is the only classical shape to have lasted several centuries after the advent of
the Han dynasty. Such "left-overs" are frequently heavily built. They stand on high,
conical, or multifaceted feet. Their shoulders are equipped with monster masks, and
the rings are connected to a chain handle which also served to keep the lid in place.
With the exception of the monster masks and a few grooves or rings encircling the
body, most vessels of this type are quite plain. Some of them, however, bear finely
incised designs influenced by the work of contemporary goldsmiths and painters.

This vessel is unique in the sense that it reproduces in gold inlay a type of decoration
which is best known by examples of the so-called "Lo-lang lacquer." On both neck
and foot bands lithe dragons, little birds, rabbits, feathered men, and other mythological
creatures are flying or running in a loose setting of clouds, small tangential circles,
and comma-shaped volutes.

Since this piece was recently acquired in Korea and shows evidence of prolonged
burial; it was probably found in a Lo-lang tomb. Lo-lang was under Chinese domination
from the first century B.C. to the fourth century A.D. The question whether this vessel
was initially imported from China or made locally in a Chinese or Korean workshop
is open, but so far no vessel of this type has been found in China proper.

PLATE LV

A. CHIAO-TOU, Ritual Lamp.

Eastern Han to Early Six dynasties
(2nd to 4th Century A.D.)
H: 6½" W: 9"   B60B968

B. PO-SHAN-LU, Incense Burner.

Han dynasty
(206 B.C. 221 A.D.)
H: 9½" D: 6½"   B60B969

The gradual secularization of bronze art did not only cause many old shapes to be abandoned or standardized, but also prompted the creation of many new ones.

(A) An oil-lamp like this one translates time-honored concepts into a new idiom. Monsters and wild beasts are replaced by a gentle and familiar fauna, complex linear effects give way to plain three-dimensional ones, latent energy explodes in expressive motions. Former casters were frequently bemused by the elementary powers of nature, and their work was ponderous if not awesome. Han artists are more interested in the ever-changing aspects and motions of earthly life, and their work is generally gay and buoyant. The slightly humoristic silhouette of this lamp is a perfect example of the syncretic Han approach where bodies and limbs are often treated cursorily in contrast to head and facial features which are rendered with great care.

(B) As a result of its conquests, the Han empire was regularly and amply supplied with aromatic woods from such countries as Parthia and Indochina. To meet an important Taoist demand, incense burners of this type were produced in vast quantities during the entire length of the period. According to contemporary texts the lower basin symbolized the Taoist Grey Jade Ocean, and the cover of the bowl represented Mount P'eng Lai, the Great Central Mountain of Taoist paradise, in the middle of that ocean. The link between the ocean and the mountain can be an animal or a human figure for by now Man is well established in his intermediate position between Heaven and Earth.

A.

B.

PLATE LVI

A. ROUND MIRROR WITH DANCING BEAR PATTERN.

Warring States Period, Ch'ang-sha Style
(4th to 3rd Century B.C.)
D: 7½"   B60B35+

B. ROUND MIRROR OF ANIMAL BELT AND NIPPLES TYPE.

Han dynasty
(206 B.C. to 221 A.D.)
D: 6¾"   B60B583

C. ROUND MIRROR OF DRAGON AND TIGER TYPE.

Eastern Han dynasty
(25 B.C. to 221 A.D.)
D: 4⅛"   B60B538

D. FIVE EMPERORS, Round Mirror, Inscribed.

Late Eastern Han or Wei Kingdom
(*ca.* 3rd Century A.D.)
D: 5⅜"   B60B1064

The beginnings of the Chinese metal mirror are in some doubt. Some place them in Shang time, others in the sixth or fifth century B.C. This artifact must be regarded as the most persistent left-over from the Bronze Age, for it was still produced in great quantities until a few decades ago.

Bronze mirrors became common articles of grave furniture toward the end of the Warring States period. Pre-Han mirrors are thin and flat. Their reverse is equipped with a small, generally fluted suspension loop and decorated in rather low relief. Starting with the Han, mirrors constituted material of high historical and archaeological significance, for they are frequently provided with dated or datable inscriptions.

(*A*) The main ornamental patterns are arranged in a not always orderly manner around the loop, and background decoration is reduced to almost indecipherably minute lines or scrolls.

(*B* and *C*) The Han perfected this tradition with their usual imperial approach. Their mirrors became bigger, thicker, and rounder, they employed better alloys and covered their best specimens with foil or gold and silver. The fragile loop handles were replaced by sturdy knobs. New designs, many of which reflected popular mythological beliefs, were now arranged in concentric bands and submitted to a strict symmetry.

(*D*) Toward the end of the period there is a tendency to crowd human and animal figures in the main register which occupies practically all the available surface as it did in Pre-Han times.

A.

C.

D.

B.

PLATE LVII

A. ROUND MIRROR WITH ANIMALS.

T'ang dynasty
(*ca.* 700 A.D.)
D: 8¼″   B60B600

B. EIGHT-LOBED MIRROR OF BIRD AND FLOWER TYPE.

T'ang dynasty
(8th Century A.D.)
D: 12″   B60B335

Although mirrors of the Sui and T'ang dynasties retain much of the basic formal characteristics of their Han and Wei predecessors, they differ from them in other ways. Concentric zones are often reduced to two or three with a sharp delineation of the central register. Geometric patterns and human representations are reduced to a minimum and give way to ornamental schemes centering on animals and plants. Gold and silver foils become increasingly popular as surface embellishments.

(*A*) This mirror with animal and vine design belongs to a well-known series which was most in fashion during the earlier part of the Tang dynasty. According to Professor A. Soper "the type grew out [partly] of the more traditional Sui scheme in which four lions . . . were disposed in quadrants reminiscent of the T-L-V type [and perhaps also partly from] magico-religious themes borrowed by the Chinese from their Central Asian neighbors."

(*B*) In describing this mirror, Professor A. Soper notes that "two 'phoenixes' with raised tails and outspread wings confront each other across the small knob. A mandarin duck, with a leaf in its beak, stands below them on axis, supported by a half-opened lotus blossom." Such mirrors, with their gentle symbolism and their quiet, slightly effeminate schemes, represent a change of taste which affirmed itself during the triumphal years of the celebrated Yang Kuei-fei.

A.

B.

PLATE LVIII

ALTAR DISH, Gilt Bronze.

T'ang dynasty
(*ca.* 8th Century A.D.)
H: 5¼″ D: 9⅛″   B60B967

This is an example of a series of new vessels used in Buddhist rituals for several centuries. Most of them—bottles, bowls, censers, and dishes—reflect foreign, and more particularly Sassanian, taste and technique.

The five-lobed body with vertical sides and a projecting rim rests on five animal legs with feline paws. The upper part of these legs are heavily decorated with a floral medallion in high relief. In particularly sophisticated specimens, the center of these flowers was probably occupied by large precious or semiprecious stones. High under the lid and between the legs are five lion heads with suspension rings in their mouths.

Legs and masks were cast separately and riveted to the body.

PLATE LIX

A. CUP, Gilt Bronze.

T'ang dynasty
(*ca.* 8th Century A.D.)
H: 2½" D: 2"   B60B819

B. BOX, Gilt Bronze.

T'ang dynasty
(*ca.* 8th Century A.D.)
H: 3¼" D: 2"   B60B669

C. BOWL ON HIGH BASE, Silver.

T'ang dynasty
(618 to 906 A.D.)
H: 2½" D: 5¼"   B60M129

The T'ang dynasty marks a turning point in the development of metal crafts—Chinese gold and silversmiths get thoroughly acquainted with the traditional techniques used by their Persian counterparts, and this helps them to free their art from former servitudes generally dictated by methods inherent in bronze casting.

The early T'ang court combines a taste for precious materials with a thirst for foreign products of quality. The command for table ware, toilette articles, and all kinds of ornaments in gold, silver or gilt bronze is enormous and Sassanian taste and techniques are evident everywhere.

Some of the most successful methods employed are raising and chasing in both silver and gold. Goldsmiths produced many articles executed in granulation, filigree, and cloisonné work with turquoise insets (Pl. LX).

(*A*) Under renewed Persian influence the old theme of the "Hunting Scene" soon experiences a lasting revival. Bare-headed hunters on horseback, wearing central Asian shoes, are chasing game in a typically simplified landscape. Taken individually, the various components of such scenes have not noticeably changed since the Han but the over all composition is radically different, and so is the underlying spirit. Here the landscape is pushed to the background as a mere setting, and the hunt is deprived of all mythological connotations. The only real Chinese notes about it are those mushroom-shaped clouds which are also to be seen on the neck zone.

(C) This is an example of Late T'ang silver work when foreign techniques and ideas have been completely assimilated and sinicized. The central motif is rendered in repoussé with detail chased on a ground of ring matting. The base and foot are soldered to the bowl.

A.

B.

C.

PLATE LX

PEACOCK, Part of Head-Dress.

T'ang dynasty
(618 to 906 A.D.)
H: 10⅛" W: 4¾"   B60M312

This frail, bouquet-like peacock is an example of T'ang court art at its best. The work is so delicate that the bird seems to be in perpetual motion like a modern mobile.

The wings and tail are made of small gold cut-outs linked together by gold threads. With the exception of the tips of the wings, feathers have been replaced by flowers and leaves. The extensive use of turquoise cloisonné and the minute granular work enlivens the surface and produces a brilliant decorative effect.

The peacock stands erect on a quatrefoil which was perhaps inspired by Han prototypes.